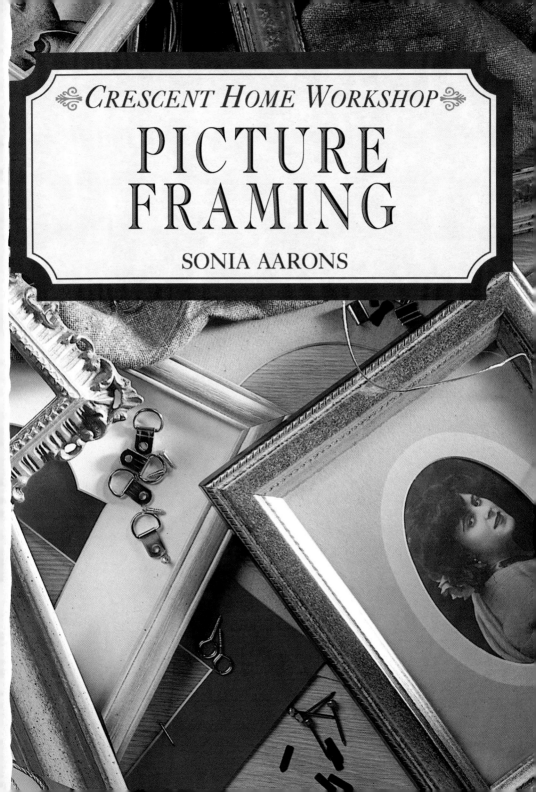

CRESCENT HOME WORKSHOP

PICTURE FRAMING

SONIA AARONS

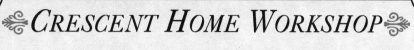

CRESCENT HOME WORKSHOP
PICTURE
FRAMING

SONIA AARONS

CRESCENT BOOKS

NEW YORK • AVENEL, NEW JERSEY

Page 2:   A grouped assortment of the framer's art.

This 1994 edition published by Crescent Books,
distributed by   Outlet Book Company, Inc.,
a Random House Company,
40 Engelhard Avenue, Avenel, New Jersey 07001

RANDOM HOUSE   New York • Toronto • London • Sydney • Auckland

Copyright © 1994   Harlaxton Publishing Limited
Copyright Design © 1994   Harlaxton Publishing Limited
2 Avenue Road, Grantham, Lincolnshire, NG31 6TA, United Kingdom.
A member of the Weldon International Group of Companies.

Publisher: Robin Burgess
Design and Coordination: Rachel Rush
Editing: Martyn Hocking
UPS Translations UK
Illustrator: Jane Pickering
Photography: Chris Allen, Forum Advertising Limited
Typesetting: Seller's, Grantham
Color Reproduction: GA Graphics, Stamford
Printing: Imago, Singapore

Title: Crescent Home Workshop - PICTURE FRAMING
ISBN: 0-517-08778-2

CONTENTS

THE
Organic
Machine

THE
Organic
Machine

Richard White

HILL AND WANG

A division of Farrar, Straus and Giroux / New York

LIBRARY OF CONGRESS CATALOGING-IN-PUBLICATION DATA
White, Richard.
The organic machine / Richard White ; consulting editor, Eric
Foner.
p.   cm. — (A critical issue)
Includes bibliographical references and index.
1. Columbia River—History. 2. Columbia River Region—History.
3. Man—Influence on nature—Columbia River. 4. Man—Influence on
nature—Columbia River Region. 5. Man—Influence of environment—
Columbia River. 6. Man—Influence of environment—Columbia River
Region.   I. Foner, Eric.   II. Title.   III. Series.
F853.W675 1995   979.7—dc20   94–46595   CIP

To Beverly,
the bravest person I know

CONTENTS

INTRODUCTION

The Columbia River has borne fewer books than barges, but its burden has been great enough so that yet another one, even one as short as this, demands justification. This is a little book with large ambitions. It is about a particular river—a stunningly beautiful river—and the people who have changed it. But it does not approach the river in the usual way. I want to examine the river as an organic machine, as an energy system which, although modified by human interventions, maintains its natural, its "unmade" qualities.

I emphasize energy because energy is such a protean and useful concept. The flow of the river is energy, so is the electricity that comes from the dams that block that flow. Human labor is energy; so are the calories stored as fat by salmon for their journey upstream. Seen one way, energy is an abstraction; seen another it is as concrete as salmon, human bodies, and the Grand Coulee Dam. I will measure the book's success by the extent to which it surprises its readers, catches them off guard, and forces them to think in new ways not merely about the Columbia but about nature and its relation to human beings and human history.

My argument in this book is that we cannot understand human history without natural history and we cannot understand natural history without human history. The two have been intertwined for millennia. As I have gotten into middle age, history has seemed less and less about things or ideas or individual persons and more and more about relationships. Nature, at once a cultural construct and a set of actual things outside of us and not fully contained by our constructions, needs to be put into human history. Nature, to paraphrase Donald Worster, is salmon swimming, the river flowing, and, I would add, humans fishing. In aiming for a relationship, I mean to do more than write a human history alongside a natural history and call it an environmental history. This would be like writing a biography of a wife, placing it alongside the biography of a husband and calling it the history of a marriage. I want the history of the relationship itself.

What I have stressed are qualities that humans and the Columbia River share: energy and work. I do not deny the huge differences between human work and the work of nature. I do not attribute either a consciousness or a purpose to nature. I do argue that it is our work that ultimately links us, for better or worse, to nature. One of the great shortcomings—intellectual and political—of modern environmentalism is its failure to grasp how human beings have historically known nature through work. Environmentalists, for all their love of nature, tend to distance humans from it. Environmentalists stress the eye over the hand, the contemplative over the active, the supposedly undisturbed over the connected. They call for human connections with nature while disparaging all those who claim to have known and appreciated nature through work and labor.

On a more mundane level, I came to this book with a dual fascination; I have long been intrigued by both salmon and dams. I first came to know salmon years ago with Indian gillnetters on the Nisqually River. The Nisqually knew salmon by catching them. They taught me, although I was too dim to recognize it then, how nature can be known through labor. My fascination with dams began the first time I saw a turbine room of a big dam. It was so obviously a human creation, and yet, paradoxically, there was virtually no visible human presence. The interior of a dam is an eerie place. The turbines turn in the unseen river; the generators produce electricity. A dam seems a piece of ghost technology. This, of course, is not true. Humans supervise the whole immense structure; without human maintenance the machinery would freeze up and cease to function. The dam would begin to self-destruct.

Being fascinated by both salmon and dams, and appreciative of the virtues of each, I have tried to write this book in quite conscious opposition to modern reductionisms: the reductions of the natural world to property, the reduction of action to discourse, of life to the market, of the great changing and multifarious planet to a stable and harmonious Nature. This is a book which seeks to blur boundaries, emphasize impurity, and find, paradoxically, along those blurred and dirty boundaries ways to better live with our dilemmas. What this book suggests is that if we want to understand what we have done and how we have acted in nature, we might want to spend more time thinking about Ralph Waldo Emerson and Lewis Mumford and less about Henry David Thoreau and John Muir. We might want to look for the natural in the dams and the unnatural in the salmon. The boundaries between the human and the natural have existed only to be crossed on the river.

I want to thank Robert Self, my research assistant on this project. His aid was invaluable. Dick Lowitt saved me a great deal of effort by allowing me access to his own files gathered in his research for his book *The New Deal and the West*. James Anderson generously allowed me to attend demonstrations of CRiSP, the most sophisticated computer model of the Columbia. Bill Rudolph sent me his own engaging, funny, and perceptive writings on the fishery disputes of the Columbia. John Findlay and Bruce Hevly, my colleagues at the University of Washington, allowed me to use their own work on Hanford, and Bruce perceptively read sections of the manuscript for me. Jay Taylor, who knows the fisheries far better than I do, read the manuscript for me, and Anne Spirn read the sections on New Deal planning. Both readings were immensely helpful; any misinterpretations and mistakes that remain are mine, not theirs. My wife, Beverly Purrington, put up with my fascination with dams, allowed me to turn "vacations" into hydroelectric tours, and read this manuscript with the kind of critical exasperation that I have come to depend on. Finally, I would like to thank Arthur Wang, who, for better or worse, persuaded me to write this book, patiently waited for it, and along with Eric Foner, the Consulting Editor of this series, provided both advice and judicious editing.

The format of this series does not include footnotes, but this manuscript is fully, indeed excessively, annotated. I will deposit a footnoted typescript of the unedited version of this manuscript in Special Collections of the University of Washington Library for those who are interested.

THE
Organic
Machine

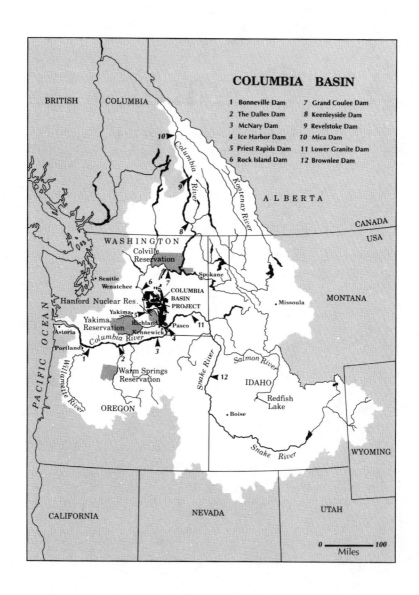

COLUMBIA BASIN

1	Bonneville Dam	7	Grand Coulee Dam
2	The Dalles Dam	8	Keenleyside Dam
3	McNary Dam	9	Revelstoke Dam
4	Ice Harbor Dam	10	Mica Dam
5	Priest Rapids Dam	11	Lower Granite Dam
6	Rock Island Dam	12	Brownlee Dam

BRITISH COLUMBIA

ALBERTA

CANADA

USA

WASHINGTON

Colville Reservation

Spokane

Seattle

Wenatchee

COLUMBIA BASIN PROJECT

Hanford Nuclear Res.

Missoula

MONTANA

PACIFIC OCEAN

Yakima

Yakima Reservation

Richland

Kennewick

Pasco

Astoria

Columbia River

Portland

Warm Springs Reservation

Salmon River

IDAHO

Redfish Lake

Boise

OREGON

Snake River

WYOMING

Willamette River

Columbia River

Kootenay River

CALIFORNIA

NEVADA

UTAH

0 ——— 100
Miles

CHAPTER 1

Knowing Nature through Labor: Energy, Salmon Society on the Columbia

I

The world is in motion. Tectonic plates drift across a spinning planet. Mountains are lifted up and eroded to the sea. Glaciers advance and retreat. All natural features move, but few natural features move so obviously as rivers. Our metaphors for rivers are all metaphors of movement: they run and roll and flow.

Like us, rivers work. They absorb and emit energy; they rearrange the world. The Columbia has been working for millennia. During the Miocene, volcanic eruptions deposited layers of basalt across the Columbia Plain. The upper Columbia cut a gutter through which it ran along the margins of the basaltic flow. At Wenatchee the rise of the Horse Heaven anticline caused the river to cut into the basalt; it drained into the Pasco basin, the lowest point on its route east of the Cascades, and emerged from the basin at the Wallula Gap. During the Pleistocene the collapse of an ice dam holding glacial Lake Missoula created the largest known freshwater flood in the earth's history. It was an afternoon's work for one of the Missoula floods to create the Grand Coulee and other rock channels of the Channeled Scablands. In those few hours it accomplished work that it would have taken the Mississippi three hundred years at full flood to duplicate. The flood rushed into the Columbia channel and finally slowed enough to create the "Portland Delta" of the Willamette lowlands. Since then ice dams have blocked the Columbia's bed, temporarily spilling the river into the Grand Coulee; mountains have slid into it, and humans have dammed it. All these changes have left work for the river to do.

For much of human history, work and energy have linked humans and rivers, humans and nature. But today, except when disaster strikes, when a hurricane hits, or earthquakes topple our creations, or when a river unexpectedly rises and sweeps away the results of our effort and labor, we forget the awesome power—the energy—of nature. There is little in our day-to-day life to preserve the connection. Machines do most of our work; we disparage physical labor and laborers. The link between our work and nature's work has weakened. We no longer understand the world through labor. Once the energy of the Columbia River was felt in human bones and sinews; human beings knew the river through the work the river demanded of them.

Early-nineteenth-century accounts of the Columbia can be read in many ways, but they are certainly all accounts of work, sweat, exhaustion, and fear. The men of the early nineteenth century who wrote the Lewis and Clark journals and the accounts of the Astorian trading post, the North West Company and Hudson's Bay Company, knew the energy of the river. They had to expend their own energy to move up, down, and across it. Alexander Ross's marvelous *Adventures of the First Settlers on the Oregon or Columbia River,* a narrative of the arrival of the Astorians and the establishment of the fur-trading outpost of Astoria in 1811, can serve as a primer on the Columbia as an energy system during a time when human beings—Indian and white—had only the wind and the strength of their own muscles to match against the powerful currents of the river.

"The mouth of the Columbia River," Ross wrote, "is remarkable for its sand bars and high surf at all seasons, but more particularly in the spring and fall, during the equinoctial gales." The shoals and sandbars at the Columbia's mouth are relics of its work and energy. In areas without strong tidal action a river deposits the load it carries to its mouth as a delta, but the Columbia emerges into the Pacific in an area of strong tides and persistent storms.

The river's current and the tides battle at the Columbia's mouth and prevent the formation of a delta. At full flood, Captain Charles Wilkes wrote in 1841, one could "scarcely have an idea of its flow how swollen it is, and to see the huge trunks of thick gigantic forests borne like chips on its bosom astonishes one." During ebb tides the river pushes its

freshwater out many miles into the sea. The tides, in turn, are felt as high as 140 miles upriver when the Columbia's water level is at its fall and winter low. This pushing and pulling produces a set of sandbars and islands at the river's mouth. Ocean currents and tides force themselves against the bars with "huge waves and foaming breakers." The result is "a white foaming sheet for many miles, both south and north of the mouth of the river, forming as it were an impracticable barrier to the entrance, and threatening with instant destruction everything that comes near it." To enter the river, ships, powered only by wind and aided by the tide, or boats and canoes powered by human muscle, had to pass through this barrier.

During the Astorians' own terrible entry into the Columbia in 1811, they sent out small boats to find a channel into the river for their ship, the *Tonquin*. In Ross's dramatic telling, the Astorians watched as the *Tonquin*'s first officer, Ebenezer Fox, protested to Captain Jonathan Thorn that the seas were "too high for any boat to live in." In reply Thorn only taunted Fox: "Mr. Fox, if you are afraid of water, you should have remained at Boston." Fox's uncle had died at the mouth of the Columbia. In despair Fox announced that he was "going to lay my bones with his." He shook hands with the Astorians and, getting into the boat, shouted, "Farewell, my friends . . . we will perhaps meet again in the next world." Fox's crew was inexperienced and the sea violent. Not one hundred yards from the ship the boat became unmanageable. The waves hit the craft broadside, whirled it like a top, and "tossing on the crest of a huge wave, [it would] sink again for a time and disappear all together." Fox hoisted a flag to signal his distress, but the *Tonquin* turned about, and they "saw the ill-fated boat no more."

Ross himself took part in a second attempt, and he discovered more immediately the experience of pitting human energy against the energy focused at the mouth of the river. As they first approached the bar with its "terrific chain of breakers," the "fearful suction or current" gripped the boat before they realized what had happened. The second officer Mr. Mumford, called for them to match their strength against that c the river and sea: "Let us turn back, and pull for your lives. Pull hard or you are all dead men." They pulled hard and survived, but th attempt to enter the river and two more failed. The *Tonquin* eventual made the passage across the bar, but only after eight men had died.

In their ordeal at the bar the Astorians had confronted storms, san

bars, and currents; men had labored and died. But wave, water, and wind—and human labor—can be represented in ways beyond the immediacy of actual experience. We can abstract them to a single entity: energy. There is a physics to the *Tonquin*'s drama at the river's mouth, and it leads outward beyond the earth to the sun and the moon. Lunar gravitation causes the tides, but virtually all the rest of the energy manifest at the Columbia's mouth originates in the sun. The sun, in effect, provides fuel for a giant atmospheric heat engine which evaporates water from the oceans and produces winds that move the moisture over land. As the clouds cool, the moisture falls as rain. Without solar energy to move the water inland and uphill, rivers would never begin; without gravity to propel the water downhill back toward the ocean, rivers would never flow. In a real sense the Columbia begins everywhere that the rain that eventually enters it falls. The Columbia gathers its water from an area of 258,200 square miles, but not all that water finds its way into the river as it flows 1,214 miles to the sea. Some of it is lost through transpiration and use in plant tissues; some is lost through evaporation.

Physicists define energy as the capacity to do work. Work, in turn, is the product of a force acting on a body and the distance the body is moved in the direction of the force. Push a large rock and you are expending energy and doing work; the amount of each depends on how large the rock and how far you push it. The weight and flow of water produce the energy that allows rivers to do the work of moving rock and soil: the greater the volume of water in the river and the steeper the gradient of its bed, the greater its potential energy.

In fact, however, neither the Columbia nor any other river realizes all of its potential energy as work. Indeed, only about 2 percent of the river's potential energy results in work: the erosion, transportation, and deposition of matter. About 98 percent of the river's kinetic energy is expended in friction as the moving water rubs against itself, its bed, and its bank. This energy is dissipated as heat within the river.

Engineers can measure the potential energy and the kinetic energy of the Columbia with some precision, but early voyagers like Ross recognized the power—the energy—by more immediate if cruder measures. They measured it by the damage it did as it threw ships or boats or bodies against rocks or sandbars. And they measured it by the work they had to perform to counter the river's work. They knew something

we have obscured and are only slowly recovering: labor rather than "conquering" nature involves human beings with the world so thoroughly that they can never be disentangled.

During the forty-two days of Ross's first trip upriver from Astoria, the river demonstrated its power again and again. The river upset the Astorians' boat; it dunked the men, drenched them, grounded them, and delayed them. But mostly the river made them work, sweat, and hurt. "On the twenty-third [of the month] . . . we started stemming a strong and almost irresistible current . . ." The "current assumed double force, so that our paddles proved almost ineffectual; and to get on we were obliged to drag ourselves from point to point by laying hold of bushes and the branches of overhanging trees . . ." "The burning sun of yesterday and the difficulty of stemming the rapid current had so reduced our strength that we made but little headway today." "We were again early at work, making the best of our way against a turbulent and still increasing current."

Ross had reached the Cascades, the rapids where the Columbia bursts out of the mountains. Above the Cascades were even worse rapids at the Dalles, and the Dalles commenced with Celilo Falls. Here the current was too strong and travelers had to portage.

Above Celilo Falls, Ross's litany of labor continued. "The current was strong and rapid the whole day." "[We] found the current so powerful that we had to lay our paddles aside and take to the lines." "The wind springing up, we hoisted sail, but found the experiment dangerous, owing to the rapidity of the current." And so they proceeded through Priest Rapids, where the "water rushes with great violence," and through lesser rapids where a whirlpool grabbed a boat, spun it several times, and sent it careening down a chain of cascades. Ross stopped at the Okanogan River. If he had gone farther, more rapids awaited: Kettle Falls, and farther still, the Dalles des Morts. The largest tributaries of the Columbia, the Snake and the Willamette, contributed falls and rapids of their own.

So thoroughly did Ross come to measure the river by the labor he pitted against it, by the feel of his body, by the difficulties it presented, that his return downstream with the river's energy speeding him back to Astoria from Fort Okanogan could be contained in a sentence. "On the twenty-sixth of February, we began our homeward journey, and spent just twenty-five days on our way back."

With so much energy deployed against them, it was remarkable that voyagers could proceed at all. The first white fur traders built what they called canoes out of cedar planks caulked with gum. Such boats could not stand the rapids. The Astorians longed for another Indian technology—the more familiar birchbark canoes of the eastern rivers. The Northwesters who succeeded the Astorians actually imported the birchbark necessary to make birchbark canoes.

Efficient movement on the river demanded not just muscle power but knowledge and art. The fur traders, fortunately, had examples of both before them. In the Indians' cedar canoes, efficiency and art met and became one. The Indians carved each of their canoes from a single log; Gabriel Franchère, another of the original Astorians, reported that the largest canoes were thirty feet long and five feet wide. And as Robert Stuart, also an Astorian, wrote: "If perfect symmetry, smoothness and proportion constitute beauty, they surpass anything I ever beheld." Some were as "transparent as oiled paper."

The art and knowledge embodied in the canoe demanded an equal knowledge of the river. Lewis and Clark were repeatedly amazed at the conditions Indians ventured out in, and William Clark had thought them "the best canoe navigators I ever Saw." Stuart concurred: The Indians were "the most expert paddle men any of us had ever seen." If the river overpowered their canoe, they would spring "into the water (more like amphibious animals than human beings), right and empty her, when with the greatest composure, they again get in and proceed." But the clearest mark of knowledge and skill was when nothing happened, when Indians knew which paths through the river were the most efficient and least demanding of human energy.

The river's lessons that the Astorians learned, the North West Company men would have to relearn. The poverty of the boats and the inability to maneuver them that the governor-in-chief of the Hudson's Bay Company, George Simpson, found on his first voyage of inspection to the Columbia posts in 1824 provoked a spluttering astonishment that still resonates in his journal. "There is not," he wrote, "a Boat at the Establishment [Fort George] fit to cross the River in bad Weather nor a person competent to sail one." Simpson's attempt to cross in a boat with rotten rigging had proceeded only a mile before everyone on board was bailing with hats and buckets. The boat struck a sandbar and drifted off, with the crew rowing madly against an outgoing tide until they "exhausted their strength at the Oars." They were only saved when the tide turned and swept them back into the river, where they made shore, abandoned the boat, and walked back to the fort. Farther upriver, however, where Canadian boatmen were more in their element, the British naturalist David Douglas could in 1826 admire the "indescribable coolness" with which Canadians shot the rapids.

The Canadians showed Douglas that the knowledge of how and where to use the boats was as important as the boats themselves; the complexities of the energy system of the river could be made to work for as well as against travelers. "Our Indians," the American explorer Charles Wilkes wrote in 1841, "cunningly kept close to the shore & thus took advantage of all the eddies." Such knowledge was initially a bodily knowledge felt and mastered through experience and labor. Even when learned from others, the messages sent through nerve and muscle constantly validated or modified acquired knowledge. Knowledge of the river was in large part knowing how its velocity varied and where it was turbulent. With proper experience, traveling against the current on the Columbia demanded less expenditure of human energy than traveling overland. The hydraulics of the river sketched out a map of energy; this geography of energy was also a geography of labor.

George Simpson saw the world with the eyes of an adventurous accountant. He gauged rivers, as he judged his men and the Indians, by the work they did, the expense they required, and the profit the company might derive from them. In 1824, on first entering the Columbia near the Cedar River, he had found the current of the Columbia "so strong that at first sight one would scarcely suppose it possible to stem it even with the Towline." But "on more attentive observation it is found that in every reach there is a strong back current or eddy which renders it easy of ascent."

The Columbia, as Simpson noted, does not travel at a constant speed along its bed. Friction divides its very current against itself. It divides it horizontally. Where the water meets earth and rock along the river's bed and banks, friction slows the current. Velocity increases away from the shore. The river's current also varies vertically. The river, in effect, is composed of layers. It is the fluid equivalent of a piece of plywood, but in the river's case each layer moves at a different velocity. The layer of greatest velocity is always below the surface. With a constant depth of flow, velocity increases toward the center of the river and rises toward the surface. Where the channel is asymmetrical, maximum velocity shifts toward the deeper side.

As Simpson noticed, the very velocity of the river created other compensatory effects that reduced human labor. Water, as a fluid, cannot resist stress. When the river's velocity reaches a certain point, the flow becomes turbulent. The layers mix; the flow at some points eddies back against the main current.

The velocity of the river changes across both space and time. When the volume of water increases in spring and summer with melting snows from the mountains, friction does not increase proportionately. The area of bank and streambed increases by a much smaller increment than does the volume of water. When deep and full, rivers run faster than when shallow. Thus the velocity of the Columbia increases in the spring and summer, and it increases the farther one goes downstream.

As every voyager on the river knew, it was not just speed that created turbulence; the flow of a river also depended on the roughness of its bed. Obstructions in its channel—rocks and boulders, trees or piers— separate its flow and create eddies. Eddies create the waves, vortices, and surges that characterize rapids. And the Columbia possessed some of the fiercest and largest rapids on the continent.

The places on the Columbia marked by the greatest turbulence and velocity formed a gauntlet through which voyagers had to pass. Roughly eight hundred years ago a three-mile chunk of Table Mountain fell into the river, blocking it entirely. Stand at Bonneville Dam and you can see the gash it left in the mountain. One hundred and fifty miles from its mouth, the river eventually cut a rocky path through the slide's outer edge, forming the Cascades. Robert Stuart described the current as that "of a Mill Sluice, and so rough that the Ocean agitated by a tempest would be but a faint comparison."

Roughly forty miles above the Cascades came the Dalles or Long Narrows, where a basalt flow constricted the Columbia. Narrowing the channel increased the velocity of the Columbia in the same way that partially blocking the outlet of a hose with your thumb increases the water's velocity. In the words of David Thompson, a North West Company man who probably knew the continent more intimately than any other human alive, the "walls of Rock contract the River from eight hundred to one thousand yards in width to sixty yards or less: imagination can hardly form an idea of the working of this immense body of water under such compression, raging and hissing as if alive." To William Clark it was an "agitated gut Swelling, boiling and Whorling in every direction." At full flood the river rose high up the narrow gorge. David Douglas saw tree trunks "3 feet in diameter . . . on the rocks, 43 feet above the present level . . . placed there by the water." Just as compression increased speed and energy, so did gravity when the incline of the river's bed steepened. Immediately above the Dalles, at Celilo Falls, cascading water increased in velocity and thus increased the amount of kinetic energy it produced.

At these places where the river narrowed and/or fell in a short distance, the river's energy was greatest. The river became dramatic and dangerous. Falls and rapids yielded disproportionate death to those inexperienced at handling boats or cedar canoes or those who chose risk over the labor of portage. There was, however, danger no matter how great the skill of the paddlers.

The early accounts of missionaries provide a grim narrative of the dangers of rivers. "The water being very high and the current strong," was the Methodist Elijah White's prologue to an 1843 accident in which a canoe carrying four whites and four Indians was swept over Willamette Falls on the Willamette River. A hopeless effort to battle the current, a "thrilling shriek" from Mrs. Rogers, and the victims were gone. Two Indians jumped and survived. Everyone else died. Five years earlier an Indian canoe carrying missionaries attempted to run the Cascades and overturned. When it was righted and brought to shore, the Indian crew found the dead body of the drowned infant son of Mrs. Elijah White in the canoe. A short time earlier a Hudson's Bay canoe with seven men was lost at the same place.

It took only bad luck, a moment's panic, or a lapse of skill for the river to claim its toll. The Dalles des Morts of the Columbia received its name in the 1820s when the river had wrecked a Hudson's Bay Company party, killing five men and reducing one survivor to cannibalism. Near the Dalles proper, nine men drowned in 1830 on a stretch of the river not considered especially dangerous. And in 1842 Father Pierre De Smet, who described the Columbia as "but a succession of dangers," watched in horror as what appears to have been the Whirlpool Rapids near Kalichen Falls swallowed a Hudson's Bay Company bateau, drowning five bargemen.

These rapids and falls created the most revealing places on the river.

They were critical sites in a geography of energy, and they were critical places in the social, cultural, and political geography humans constructed. A scholar needs to consider them at least as carefully and from as many angles as a boatman preparing to run them.

As we now understand rivers, they seek the most efficient and uniform expenditure of energy possible. Rivers constantly adjust; they compensate for events that affect them. They are, in this sense, historical: products of their own past history. "The river channel," concluded one geomorphologist, is "a form representing the most efficient—in terms of energy utilization—geometry capable of accommodating the sum total of the means and extremes of variability of flow that have occurred in that channel throughout its history."

Where obstacles slow rivers, rivers try to restore an even velocity; where the gradient increases or the channel constricts, rivers try to widen or build up their bed. The Columbia ceaselessly worked to widen the Dalles and it responded to Celilo Falls by working to downcut the falls and erode the plunge pools until the falls themselves eventually would even out and disappear. When an obstacle such as a beaver dam or a hydraulic dam slows a river's current, for example, its speed and energy decrease. The river drops part of its load—the material it works to move. It gradually builds up its own bed and increases its gradient, thus increasing its speed and its kinetic energy. Eventually it will remove the obstacle.

In the long run the river's work of eliminating obstructions aids the human work of moving up and down rivers. But in the short run rapids and falls demand greater expenditures of human energy to counter the river's energy. This combination of energies bonded the material and social; the natural and cultural intertwined. The geography of energy intersected quite tightly with a geography of danger and a human geography of labor. Precisely where the river expended its greatest energy, humans had to expend the most labor and confront the greatest danger.

At the falls and rapids travelers had to portage. Indians living at the Cascades had canoes at either end of the portages, but travelers had to carry their cargo and either tow or carry their boats. It was hard and demanding work. Portaging the Cascades brought Lewis and Clark much "difficulty and labour," cost them a pirogue, and left their men "so much fatigued" that they granted them a respite. The missionary

Mrs. Elijah White, whose baby drowned at the Cascades, had gladly reembarked two-thirds through the portage because she and David Leslie "with wet feet and fatigue were very uncomfortable." Going upstream, everyone had to portage; going downstream, danger could be substituted for labor.

The Cascades and the Dalles were the most dangerous points on the river and the longest portages. At the Cascades—which one of the literary Astorians described as "that rocky and dangerous portage"—the "laborious task of carrying" made clear the distinction between the work of the river and the work of human beings. In one sense, the expenditure of energy by human workers was as natural as the energy of the river, but human work was socially organized and given cultural meaning. The Cascades and the Dalles, for example, bared class divisions among the Astorians and revealed their relation to work and power. Ross, "not being accustomed myself to carry," instead stood armed as a sentinel against the Indians, but with those subordinate to him "wearied to death," he took up a load. The first ascent left him breathless and able to "proceed no farther." He hired an Indian to carry the load, and the Indian proceeded "full trot" across the portage, only to pitch the pack of tobacco over a two-hundred-foot precipice at the end. He and fifty others laughed uproariously as Ross scrambled to retrieve the load. The joke was about work and power, weakness and dominance, all of which were physical and social.

The river demanded energy to match its energy, and this shaped and revealed the organization of work. The necessity of portages and the limits of human labor caused the Hudson's Bay Company to transport all its goods in ninety-pound packages. The expenditure of labor in carrying these packages involved numerous acts of calculation, conflict, abuse, and cooperation. In these acts a social order became transparent.

If all journeys were downstream, if there had been no rapids or falls, then the human relations on the early-nineteenth-century river would have been different. The labor white men expended in the ascent forced them into close contact with Indians. The knowledge that in passing upstream they had to travel close to shore to take advantage of back-currents encouraged efforts to accommodate Indians. David Thompson, the remarkable North West Company explorer who descended the Columbia just as the Astorians were arriving at its mouth, succinctly calculated the social result of this mix of river energy and human labor when he explained why he stopped to smoke and exchange gifts with the Sanpoils as he passed downstream.

> My reason for putting ashore and smoking with the Natives, is to make friends with them, against my return, for in descending the current of a large River, we might pass on without much attention to them; but in returning against the current, our progress will be slow and close along the shore, and consequently very much in their power; whereas staying a few hours, and smoking with them, while explaining to them the object of my voyage makes them friendly to us.

Passage along the river was, Thompson realized, not just physical; it was social and political. Social and political rituals were as necessary as labor to move against the current. Indians expected gifts and ritual at the portages. The failure of whites to meet such expectations brought conflict from the time of the Lewis and Clark expedition until the 1820s.

In English the words "energy" and "power" have become virtually interchangeable. Horsepower is, for example, a technical measure of energy. But we also speak metaphorically of the power of the state. Thompson spoke of being "in the power" of the Indians. The conflation is partially metaphorical, but it also arises because both meanings involve the ability to do work, to command labor. To be powerful is to be able to accomplish things, to be able to turn the energy and work of nature and humans to your own purposes.

We conflate energy and power, the natural and the cultural, in language, but they are equally mixed as social fact at the rapids and portages. The energy system of the Columbia determined where humans would portage, but human labor created the actual route of the portage, and human social relations determined its final social form and outcome. The Dalles, per se, did not cause Ross's dilemma. Ross's humiliation was an incident of power. Human labor would later make the Dalles and the Cascades the sites of dams that produced energy—power; they were, however, long before this, sites at which humans contested over social power—the ability to gain advantage from the labor of others.

Spatial arrangements matter a great deal in human history. They reveal the social arrangements that help produce them. The repeated conflicts at the Dalles and the Cascades revolved around a particular organization of space. Whites regarded the space at the Cascades and the Dalles as open, as culturally empty. Indians regarded it as full. In a space that brought together many different peoples, Indians expected gifts to mediate and smooth passages through this social maze. Too often whites replaced gifts with force; they resented what they perceived as theft and pillage. The space became uniquely violent.

II

Examining how humans moved on the river provides one angle of vision on the rapids and falls of the Columbia; examining how salmon moved up and down the river provides a second, equally revealing, perspective. It was, after all, the salmon that brought thousands of Indians to the Cascades, to the Dalles and Celilo Falls, to Priest Rapids and Kettle Falls.

As much as wind, wave, and current, salmon were part of the energy system of the Columbia. Salmon are anadromous fish: they live most of their adult life in the ocean but return to the stream of their birth to spawn since the Columbia does not provide sufficient food to support the salmon born in its tributaries. The precise timing of the movement of young salmon to the sea depends on the species, but eventually all except the kokanee (a form of sockeye which, although nonanadromous, retains the genetic potential to become so) make their way to the ocean. During their time at sea Columbia salmon harvest the far greater solar energy available in the Pacific's food chain and, on their return, make part of that energy available in the river. By intercepting the salmon and eating them, other species, including humans, in effect capture solar energy from the ocean. Salmon thus are a virtually free gift to the energy ledger of the Columbia. They bring energy garnered from outside the river back to the river.

For salmon the rapids and the falls represent obstacles that force them to expend energy, but to the Indians the combination of salmon and rapids and falls seemed providential. In 1811 Gabriel Franchère traveled with one of the sons of Concomly, the leading Chinook chief on the lower Columbia. He told Franchère that in perfecting creation Ekan-unum (Coyote) had "caused rocks to fall in the river so as to obstruct it and bring the fish together in one spot in order that they might be caught in sufficient quantities." On the Columbia, where the river was the most turbulent the fishing was best. Rapids and waterfalls forced fish into narrow channels; they forced salmon toward the surface. And as the fish became concentrated and visible, they became more vulnerable to capture.

At the rapids human art and technology altered the river to increase the difficulties for fish. At low water in early May, for example, the Nespelems and Sanpoils built weirs to deflect fish toward artificial channels cleared at certain points in the rapids. The bottoms of the channels were lined with white quartz to make the fish more visible. On smaller tributaries, the Indians built weirs to block the fish until their harvest was complete. At Kettle Falls the Indians fixed timber frames in the rocks of the falls and from them they hung huge willow baskets, ten feet in diameter and twelve feet deep. Leaping salmon would strike the frames and fall into the baskets, where waiting fishermen clubbed and removed them. A single such basket could supposedly yield five thousand pounds of fish a day at the height of the runs.

Robert Stuart described how, at the Dalles, Cathlakaheckits and Cathlathalas built scaffoldings which extended out over the water. "The places chosen are always a point where the water is strongest, and if possible a mass of rock near the projection between which and the shore the Salmon are sure to pass, to avoid the greater body of the current." From the platforms fishermen extended dip nets, and during the peak of the run "the operator hardly ever dips his nett without taking one and sometimes two Salmon, so that I call it speaking within bounds when I say that an experienced hand would by assiduity catch at least 500 daily."

The human energy expended to obtain salmon did not dependably yield a proportionate return of caloric energy from the fish. Salmon do not bestow their gift of energy evenly. Salmon cease feeding when they enter freshwater and live off the fat they have formed while feeding in the ocean. Because salmon burn stored calories to progress against the current, they lose caloric value as they proceed upstream. Early travelers along the river noted the changing quality of the salmon. Descending the river, David Thompson did not find fat salmon until he was near present-day Pasco. Thompson found the Indians taking salmon as high up as the Arrow Lakes, but "they were very poor, necessity made them eatable."

Thompson was not being an epicure. His own body, needing calories to provide energy to do the work the Columbia demanded, craved fat salmon for a reason and rightly gauged its quality. A salmon caught at the mouth had 100 percent of its original caloric value. A salmon caught by the Wishrams at the Dalles had roughly 88 percent. A salmon caught by the Nez Percés near the Snake River had 52 percent. A salmon caught by the Kutenais on the Kootenay River at Nelson or Windemere, British Columbia, had only 25 percent.

The gifts salmon gave varied temporally as well as spatially. The extraordinary yields at the fisheries Stuart mentioned were fleeting. There was a seasonality to the river flow and fish runs that neither art nor knowledge could overcome. During spring flood in late May and June, many sites at the rapids could not be fished at all. The salmon set other limits. Four species of salmon (Oncorhynchus), as well as the steelhead trout (Oncorhynchus mykiss), spawn in the Columbia and its tributaries, and there is some evidence that a fifth species, pink salmon, once did so. Before their late-nineteenth- and twentieth-century de-cline, they returned to the Columbia in astonishing numbers, but they did not go everywhere nor did they come evenly. All species passed through the lower river, but at each tributary some spawners separated from the main run; the size of a run decreased as it proceeded up the Columbia.

The largest salmon species was the chinook or king salmon, and it was the chinook that came up the river in the greatest numbers. They actually came in three separate runs: spring, summer, and fall. Each run differed not only in its timing but in its combination of spawning areas, size of fish, and life history. Originally, the spring chinook run was the largest and, for most Indians, the most critical. The first fish might enter the river in February, but the Chinook Indians told Lewis and Clark that they arrived in significant numbers in April. Robert Stuart said spring chinooks reached the Dalles in mid-May, with the greatest numbers coming over the next two months.

Subsequent runs shaded into each other. The spring run of chinook (O. tshawytscha) merged into the summer run and the summer into the fall. Sockeye or blueback (O. nerka), which spawn in lakes, come in late summer and early fall, and the coho or silver *(O. kisutch)* arrive in the fall. The chum or dog salmon *(O. keta)*, the least desirable species, first enters the river in October and spawns largely in the lower tributaries below the Dalles. The steelhead *(O. mykiss)*, an oceangoing trout which spawns and returns to the sea, has a summer and winter run. The size of each of these runs fluctuates from year to year.

The seasonality of salmon and the geography of energy that concentrated fishing sites meant that during a relatively short span of time a single place provided a sizable portion of the total annual caloric intake of Indian peoples on the Columbia. At the Dalles the Wishrams and Wascos derived between 30 and 40 percent of their annual energy requirements from salmon; at the other extreme, farther upriver, the Kutenais, Flatheads, and Coeur d'Alenes obtained 5 percent or less.

Taking so many salmon in so short a time, however, meant that the salmon were worthless unless preserved. Preserving fish on the Columbia meant drying them, and this demanded a second convergence of labor and energy. Women's work preserved the fish men caught. On the lower river fish often had to be smoked to be dried, but at the Dalles and above Indians could rely on solar energy—the direct heat of the sun—to dry the fish they split and set out on racks.

As the salmon dwindle and environmental crises deepen, there is an understandable tendency to romanticize and even invent pasts in which the planet was nurturing and humans simply accepting and grateful. And the Columbia, with the annual passage of millions of fish, invites such images. Salmon have sustained culturally rich human communities whose way of life stretches back over five thousand years.

But the people who awaited the salmon were not simple fisherfolk gratefully taking the bounty of their mother earth. Culturally, they made no assumptions about the inevitability of the salmon's return. Their rituals, their social practices, their stories all recognized the possibility that the fish would fail to appear. They waited for salmon not with faith but with anxiety. Depending on how long Indian cultural memories extended, they had good reason to worry. When Table Mountain slid into the river eight hundred years ago and formed a huge lake, it almost certainly cut off all the people upriver from the salmon runs until the river broke through.

In the myths of the river there is a recurring motif of a time when

sisters imprisoned the salmon—sometimes within a lake or pond, sometimes behind a dam—and how they are freed by Coyote, the lecherous
and often foolish culture hero. Coyote, who defecates so he can consult
his feces whenever he needs advice, often uses either the wisdom of
women or the tools of women—digging sticks—to take the salmon from
the sisters. Indians usually put the site of this dam near the Cascades.

In these stories the women who prevent the coming of the salmon
are identified with birds. They are often *wi'dwid*, a Sahaptin word
usually translated as swallows, but which also can refer to water snipes
or wild ducks. Sometimes it is eagle people who imprison the salmon.
Sometimes it is the sandpipers. But as the Wishram story makes explicit,
the connection is with a bird whose migration coincides with the spring
arrival of the chinook, or as among the Sanpoils, with birds who live
by the water and eat fish. In another Wishram myth Dove is Salmon's
wife. "Whenever the salmon comes, they kill him at Wishram, and
then the dove cries."

This connection between women, birds, salmon, and a time when
the salmon did not come was ritually reenacted each year along the
river. When the salmon ran and the birds returned, the activities of
women became circumscribed. Space reflected and structured power
as men controlled access to the fish. Among the Sanpoils and Nespelems
men prohibited women not only from visiting fish traps but also from
crossing or using trails that led to them. Women could not take water
from a stream that contained a fish trap. They had to remain several
paces away from the distributing center which contained the common
catch. The taboos affected all women, but their prime object was menstruating women, whose contact with water or salmon could cause the
run to cease.

The blood of menstruating women was not unique in its power to
offend salmon. Any bone had the same effect. So did internal organs.
So, too, did the death of a fisherman. David Thompson, watching the
fishing at Kettle Falls, reported that neither the scales nor the bowels
of cleaned fish were thrown back into the water. If a speared fish escaped,
fishing was done for the day. When the spear of one fisherman came
too close to the skull of a dead dog, it was polluted and fishing ceased
until spear and spearman were ritually purified. Thompson himself was
inclined to dismiss all this as superstition, but when one of Thompson's

Canadians threw the bone of a dead horse into the river, he reported that the fish vanished. An Indian had to dive down and retrieve the bone. A few hours later the salmon returned.

But the fishery in actual practice was about doing everything that the taboos prohibited: it was about shedding blood; it was about taking what was inside living things—blood, bone, and organs—and putting it outside. It was about the death necessary to sustain life. And the rituals acknowledged this and compensated for it by treating with reverence and respect, in a controlled ceremonial context, those things which, if uncontrolled, could cause the salmon to disappear.

When the salmon first appeared, Indians shed its blood ritually; they consumed it ritually; they preserved the bones. Sometimes the ritually treated blood and bones were restored to the river. To catch salmon, the Astorians had to observe ritual prohibitions. They could not cut salmon crosswise, and if cooked, the salmon had to be consumed before sundown.

The rituals along the Columbia took the biological necessity of obtaining the caloric energy needed to live and elaborated it into a web of social meaning and power that took on consequences of its own. Both men and women caught and ate salmon, but not equally. Ritual restricted the movements and actions of women far more than those of men. The rituals connected the taking of fish with the privileged position of men over women and reinforced that position. They gave men the credit for bringing salmon to the people and placed most of the burden of the failure of the salmon runs on women.

But the elaboration went further than this. In this most critical of times, many groups created a salmon chief, a man who had the power to regulate the fisheries by deciding when fishing began and ended. That the salmon chief had the power to control the timing of human work at the fishery is so clear that we tend to neglect the way in which that chief also indirectly controlled access to space at the fishery.

The acts by which salmon swim upstream, are caught by human beings, and are eaten take place in a temporal sequence, but they are also movements through space. For millennia their culminating moments tended to take place at specific sites: salmon were caught at the Dalles or the Cascades or Celilo Falls; they spawned in the specific stream of their birth.

Humans, too, lived at specific sites and moved through space in a predictable manner. The lower Columbia River valley was one of the most densely populated areas of aboriginal North America. The names of the peoples who lived there are, however, hardly familiar even to scholars who study Indian peoples. There were Chinooks and Clatsops and also Kathlamets and Wahkiakums near the mouth of the river. Katskanies and Cowlitzes a little farther upstream. Then come Skillutes, Kalamas, Quthlapottles, Clannarminnamons, Multnomahs, Tilla-mooks, Shotos, Clanninatas, Cathlahnaquiahs, Cathlacommahtups, and many, many more, before the last of the predominantly Chinookan speakers, the Wascos and Wishrams, yielded to Sahaptin speakers at Celilo Falls. The names, drawn largely from Lewis and Clark, the Astorians, and other early voyagers on the river, form a lexographic thicket. Sometimes they signify a town or village; sometimes a group of towns or villages; sometimes they refer to what whites regarded as a tribe, sometimes to the people living in a geographic region.

But all these towns and villages, all these "tribes" and territories, were porous. The lower Columbia was not a world of tribes. The basic social unit was the village or town organized around a core population of related males. People ebbed and flowed in and out of these settlements according to season. Summer sites attracted families related through women. Such movements seasonally fragmented winter villages as people moved toward the Columbia in summer; away from it in winter. People could not go wherever they chose. Space was not empty or free. Movements demanded connections, and the strongest connections came through the out-marriage of women. Kin connections secured usufructary rights at fishing places and at wapato grounds. This was a society of dense networks of relations, and the salmon fisheries formed a basic node where the lines of human relationships intersected. The possibility of taking salmon in large numbers drew people to the fisheries from a wider region. When the salmon ran, thousands of people flocked to the Columbia fisheries from the interior. At the Dalles the permanent population of roughly 600 swelled to as high as 3,000 during the peak of the fishery.

As nodes where the lines of human relationships clustered, the fish-eries revealed a regional organization. They marked, first of all, a broad division between summer and winter towns and villages. The activities that took place at the summer sites emphasized kinship ties through women. They were materially central, the sites of fishing and food gathering.

The internal spacing of activities at the summer fishing sites is also revealing. It is impossible now to re-create in detail the spatial organization of the Dalles or the Cascades. No one mapped them or tapped human memories to demarcate them before they vanished under the waters of the dams. But such maps of memory do remain for Celilo Falls, which was really the beginning of the Dalles. The falls was among the most densely named and intimately known places on the river. The names grew from human labor. Celilo Falls is gone now, buried since 1956 beneath the waters of the Dalles Dam, but once it was thick with specifically known and bounded human spaces. At Celilo, Sahaptin fishers named places where people cast gill nets when the river ran normally; others named places to cast nets when it ran high. At *tayxay-tapamá* there was a bed of pale flat stones under clear water which made the fish stand out for spear fishing. Where the river fell at *sapawilalatatpamá*, men could dipnet leaping salmon. At *áwxanayčaš* ("standing place") seven men could stand with their dip nets on twenty-foot poles to dip into the rushing current. Nearly every rock and island in the falls suitable for fishing acquired a name.

Such spatial divisions both made visible and reproduced the social structure of the Chinookans and Sahaptins who fished the rapids. Just below Celilo Falls, at the Wishram villages on the north bank of the Dalles, such fishing stations were owned by groups of relatives who controlled access. Each group seems to have had a station for using dip nets in summer, for spearing in the fall, and for seining.

To watch such fisheries would be to watch an intricate series of convergences among the energy of the river, the work of salmon, and the labor of humans. It would be to see how humans socially and culturally organized this labor and to glimpse how people were connected and ranked. The spatial arrangements created maps of energy, maps of labor, and maps of meaning. Each of these places was unique. They were bounded spaces which, in Michel Foucault's words, were "irreducible to one another and absolutely not superimposable on one another." There was only one *Awxanaycas* at Celilo and which seven men stood there was socially determined.

In this world the human and the natural were tightly linked, but one did not determine the other. The social organization of Indians was not reducible to control of the rapids or access to salmon; there were no recorded "tribal" conflicts over resources or territory. Geography and nature influenced without determining culture.

At the rapids the intersection of labor and nature produced wealth. There is no doubt about that. The abundance was readily apparent to the first whites. Lewis and Clark saw, in Clark's fractured spelling, "emenc quantites of dried fish." They presumed the fish were for trade, but they could not figure out who bought them.

Lewis and Clark presumed a market which reduced everything in the world to an equivalence. Making things equivalent did not mean making everything equal in value, but it did mean that any good could theoretically be traded for any other good. But this was not true on the Columbia. Food normally moved only in exchange for other types of food. The caloric energy of fish was the great wealth of the fishing places, but it could not readily be translated into other forms of wealth with higher prestige value. Food had a different social meaning than did slaves, dentalium shells, or canoes.

Exchanges of food suggested an ongoing relationship rather than a single act in which a person sought advantage. And thus at the Dalles, the great mart of the Columbia, fish occupied only a limited sector of exchange. Those who flocked there to trade came for horses, buffalo robes, beads, cloth, knives, and axes. They traded and gambled while the huge yields of fish supported their numbers. Those who came for fish came because they had the kin connections that allowed them to share the fishery and take their own fish. They created the huge stocks of pounded and dried salmon that Lewis and Clark saw. This salmon would see them through the winter. And because the fish had expended some of their fat in reaching the Dalles, salmon dried there had a lower oil content and would keep better than fish caught lower down. This was prime dried salmon and would be traded, usually for other types of food, up and down the river.

At the Dalles and the Cascades ownership of a particular fishing site did not automatically translate into wealth. The fish belonged to the fishermen who caught them, but old men could freely take the fish they required for their meals. And strangers and relatives both could claim some of the bounty of the catch. Many of the strangers who concentrated at the Dalles during the fishing season never fished, nor did they lay in a supply of fish.

And fish, in any case, had little to do with the competitive social rankings of people and villages apparent in ceremonies such as the potlatch. It was wealth in scarce and valuable goods—in slaves from more distant peoples or dentalium shells or trade goods—that buttressed such rankings. Food, usually abundant and of lesser prestige, could not normally obtain such things. The Dalles and Celilo, the great fisheries and site of this exchange of wealth, thus ranked below the winter towns and villages lower down the Columbia. The winter villages of the lower river where related males lived were the sites of riskier and higher-prestige activities: slave raids, warfare, and religious performances.

The whites partially changed these relations. They offered nonfood valuables for food. And Indians, hesitantly at first, made an exception for them. Ross and Franchère, like Lewis and Clark before them, described the initial difficulty of trading for fish or other food. Fish eventually moved in exchange for the valuables whites offered, but thirty years after the arrival of the Astorians, Charles Wilkes reported that at the Cascades the Indians "refuse to sell any Salmon until after the first run and then always without the heart they have many super-stitions in relation to them . . ."

III

There was a final geography of energy on the Columbia, an interior geography of the human body itself. The human body always forms an exterior geography of signs; a map of meaning. On the lower Columbia, for example, a flattened head denoted freedom, a round head slavery. A dentalium shell in the septum told of wealth or status. But within the body, beneath such signs, we form a space in which other organisms live. Such organisms can be as lethal to us as we are to the salmon; they can mark our bodies with other signs.

A sustained note of bewilderment and subdued horror entered the journals of Lewis and Clark when they reached the Dalles. The eyes of the Indians triggered it. Many of the Indians were blind, or nearly so. Many of them, indeed, had lost one of their eyes. Clark, always ready to venture a cause, thought it was the amount of time they spend on the water; the reflection of the sun must have destroyed their sight. But he himself was not satisfied. He returned to the subject again and again. Part of the problem could have been trachoma, but part was smallpox, which can cause scarring of the cornea and blinding. In April 1806 when Clark asked about the decline of a village, an old man exhibited a woman around thirty years of age who was scarred by small-pox as a small child. Her body served as a calendar of the disease. Clark estimated the last arrival of the smallpox as twenty-eight or thirty years earlier.

The smallpox that marked this young woman's body left even deeper cultural markings among the Chinooks. In 1811, that fateful year in which the Astorians and David Thompson established a permanent non-Indian presence on the Columbia, an odd premonitory episode occurred. Soon after the arrival of the Astorians, two Algonquian-speaking Indians from east of the Rockies arrived at the mouth of the Columbia. Theirs was an unrecorded journey certainly as epic as that of the Astorians or of David Thompson. The husband, Kocomenepeca, was "very shrewd and intelligent" and provided the Astorians with val-uable information about the interior. The pair accompanied the first party of Astorians to go up the Columbia.

When David Thompson arrived at Astoria, he saw the couple, but he did not recognize them until he began his return trip in company with the Astorians. At the Cascades the young man, "well dressed in leather, carrying a Bow and Quiver of Arrows, with his Wife, a young woman in good clothing, came to my tent door and requested me to give them my protection." The man, Thompson realized, was a woman "who three years ago was the wife of Boisverd, a canadian and my servant." Thompson had requested that Boisverd dismiss her because of her loose conduct, and he had done so. She had become a prophetess, "declared her sex changed, that she was now a Man, dressed, and armed herself as such, and also took a young woman to Wife, of whom she pretended to be very jealous."

The women carried with them a letter. They told Indians of the Columbia that it came from a white chief who desired to fill their every want. But white traders, instead of bestowing presents on the Indians as the chief wished, cheated them and demanded payment for the goods. The women themselves received presents for bringing such tidings. They possessed, Ross reported, twenty-six horses, many of them loaded with robes, leather, and dentalium shells.

But these were not the only stories the prophetess told. She had, when with the Chinooks, predicted a recurrence of epidemics "which made some of them threaten her life, and she found it necessary to return to her own country . . ." This is why she sought Thompson's protection. And she immediately had need of it, for at the Cascades the Indians told Thompson that Kocomenepeca had told them that the whites had brought the smallpox to destroy them, and "also [that] two men of enormous size . . . are on their way to us, overturning the Ground, and burying all the Villages and Lodges underneath it." Thompson reassured them, promising that the skies and ground would not change. As it was in the days of their grandfathers, it would be in the days of their grandsons.

Kocomenepeca was a better prophet than Thompson. Disease did come, and big men would eventually come and bury the villages under earth and water. By and large the people below the Dalles were reduced to remnant groups by 1834. As Lewis and Clark had discovered, the Chinooks had reason to fear. The smallpox had already struck twice, forcing the abandonment of entire towns.

But it was malaria, brought up from California by returning Hudson's Bay Company fur brigades in 1830, that catastrophically rearranged the human geography of the river. The mosquito that carried the disease (Anopheles malculipennis) was rare along the coast and scarce east of the Cascades, but where the mosquito thrived on the lower Columbia death rates reached 90 percent. The seasonal cycles of the lower river became a trap as the summer search for wapato led women into the wetlands where wapato and mosquitoes thrived. In September 1830, John McLoughlin noted that "the Intermittent Fever is making a dreadful havoc among the Natives." He reported that malaria had carried off 75 percent of the Indians around Fort Vancouver. The survivors congregated at the fort. They gave as a reason that they knew if they died the Hudson's Bay Company men would bury them. Reluctantly, McLoughlin had them driven away. His own people were so sick that he could barely attend to them.

After that malaria came annually. It devastated the villages along the Willamette in 1831 and left towns and villages empty and deserted and the shores of the Columbia strewn with dead from Oak Point to the

Dalles. By 1835, the American fur trader and entrepreneur Nathaniel Wyeth was writing from the once thickly settled Wapato (Sauvie) Island in the Columbia that "a mortality has carried off to a man its inhabitants and there is nothing to attest that they ever existed except their decaying houses, their graves and their unburied bones of which there are heaps." Mortality from a single epidemic was never so high above the Dalles, but following contact with whites epidemics repeatedly cut into the population. The population of the Columbian Plateau fell by nearly 50 percent between contact and 1855. By 1875 the total loss was close to two-thirds.

The whole world changed. The Columbia continued to flow and the salmon to swim; humans continued to labor—all the elements of the energy system remained intact, but their relation was altered. Below the Cascades the intricately arranged human geography of the river's borders largely vanished. The salmon encountered fewer human obstacles on their return upstream.

Fishing pressure at the Dalles and the Cascades diminished as the number of fishermen declined. Nathaniel Wyeth had cautioned that "the impression of the vast quantity of salmon in the Columbia arises from not considering the vast number of Indians employed in catching what is seen" (sic). But as disease eliminated Indians, probably more salmon spawned in the rivers and streams than ever before. White fishermen did not quickly replace Indian fishermen. Wyeth's own attempts to go into the business of salting and exporting salmon failed. The Hudson's Bay Company's harvest of the fish was only a minimal debit against the millions that Indians no longer harvested. But like Charles Wilkes, those arriving on the river could not help but think that in the future Columbia salmon would and should "afford a large source of profit to its Settlers."

Like the prophetess Kocomenepeca, Samuel Parker, a missionary sent by the American Board of Commissioners for Foreign Missions, arrived in the midst of change and envisioned a drastically altered Columbia. He prophesied matter-of-factly. He did not call upon giants to effect this transformation, but he thought in terms of energy and labor equal to that of Kocomenepeca's giants.

The power of the Columbia astonished Parker as thoroughly as it had astonished the Astorians. He marveled at the river's "boiling eddies and the varying currents." The skill of the Indians at managing the rapids dazzled him. But this convergence of natural energy and human energy became for Parker almost a sideshow. He foresaw the possibility of new convergences of the river's energy and human labor which would transform the Columbia, its tributaries, and the lives humans lived alongside it.

The question often arose in my mind, can this section of the country ever be inhabited, unless these mountains shall be brought low, and these valleys shall be exalted? But they may be designed to perpetuate a supply of wood for the wide-spread prairies; and they may contain mines of treasures, which, when wrought, will need these forests for fuel, and these rushing streams for water power.

At Celilo Falls he saw a "situation for water power equal to any in any part of the world." At the Willamette Falls, Parker found the scenery had "much to charm and interest," but what gripped him was the opportunity to harness the Willamette's energy.

The opportunities here for water power are equal to any that can be found. There cannot be a better situation for a factory village than on the east side of the river, where a dry wide-spread level extends some distance, and the basaltic shores form natural wharves for shipping.

When Joel Palmer arrived at Oregon City at the Willamette Falls in 1845, the first marks of the new order had appeared. Dr. John Mc-Loughlin, the pillar of the old Hudson's Bay Company, had taken a donation claim and laid out a townsite. He had also finished a mill (contemplated and begun much earlier) which would "compare well with most of the mills in the states." The Methodists had built a second mill. The water of falls "constitute[d] great water privileges for propelling machinery"; they powered the mills, each of which served as both gristmill and sawmill. It was a small beginning, but Palmer jumped quickly to a grander future, for "Nature rarely at any one point concentrates so many advantages for the erection and support of a great commercial and manufacturing city." Abundant waterpower, prime farmland, a "navigable river to bring the raw material to the manufactories, and when manufactured to carry the surplus to the Pacific, whence it can easily be taken to the best markets the world affords." Palmer was wrong in the details—Oregon City would not be the center of Oregon—but he was right enough in envisioning along the Columbia and its tributaries a new energy regime, a new geography, and a new relationship between human labor and the energy of nature.

CHAPTER 2
Putting the River
to Work

I

Nineteenth-century Americans gave contests between machines and nature an epic quality. They measured progress by the results. Machines stood as both the agents and the symbols of their conquest of nature. The machine, a product of their minds and hands, was their surrogate in what seemed a simple opposition of the mechanical and the natural. Machines could exert far greater force than human bodies alone could muster. Machines replaced bodies. Machines overcame nature.

But what seemed simple was not. From one perspective machines seemed unnatural, but from another they seemed but a new manifestation of natural forces. The natural and mechanical separated only to be intertwined.

In the summer of 1894 the greatest recorded flow in the Columbia's history drowned the rapids at the Cascades, allowing steamboats to proceed upriver—*if* they could overcome the current in full flood. The famed Clatsop "Indian captain" Michell Martineau tried to run the stern-wheeler *D. S. Baker* upriver from Portland through the Cascades. But even with cables pulling the boat from the head of the rapids and the boiler at full pressure, the power of the river brought the *D. S. Baker* to a shuddering standstill. Captain Martineau gave up. "No boat nor man," he said, "can turn this trick."

The struggle seemed elemental: human contrivance against natural power. Nature won a round, but, a century later, the defeat of the

D. S. Baker becomes merely a sign of our own progress. We read
Martineau's words ironically, since tugboats and barges now "turn this
trick" daily.

The *D. S. Baker* was a machine, a stern-wheeler, whose power came
from wood burned in its boiler. By the late nineteenth century humans
approached the river largely through such machines. Earlier, machines
had rarely mediated the human relation to the Columbia. Humans had
long applied art and technology to the river (Chinook canoes, Sahaptin
dip nets, Yankee sailing ships were certainly all clever and artful), but
the power deployed remained organic, that of muscle and wind. The
1830s, when the Hudson's Bay Company harnessed steam to power its
steamship and falling water to power its mills, provided a glimpse of a
different future in which machines would counter the power of the
river and make it work for human purposes.

Steamships were the clearest sign of a new age. The British scientist
James Joule had unraveled the physics of steam engines, showing that
heat and mechanical energy are interchangeable. Fuel in a furnace
produced heat that turned water to steam that could drive cylinders and
turn wheels. By turning a paddle wheel, steam engines moved boats
upriver. In 1850, John Ainsworth, later head of the Oregon Steam
Navigation Company, took his first passage upriver from Astoria on,
fittingly enough, the ninety-foot-long side-wheeler *Columbia*. Steam
would eventually make Ainsworth the most powerful man in Oregon,
but in 1850 it barely got him to Portland. The boat was out two nights
on the hundred-mile trip. Ainsworth slept on deck, prudently keeping
the paddle box between himself and the river since the boat "would list
several streaks if a passenger would go from one side to another."

In hindsight, machines like the *Columbia* seem mere toys, possessing
barely enough power to counter the river. In 1851 the captain of the
Venture neglected to check with his engineer before launching that
boat on its maiden voyage at the Cascades. For "want of sufficient steam
to stem the current," the *Venture*, which intended to go forward, drifted
backward. Its voyage upriver became a voyage downriver and over the
falls at the upper Cascades.

The same limitations of the new machinery strike us when we consider the canneries that crowded the Columbia's shores. The very rich-
ness of the fishery initially limited the inroads of machines. The many
different varieties of chinook salmon meant a large variation in the size

of the fish. The so-called iron chink, a machine that butchered the fish and replaced Chinese workers elsewhere in the Northwest, could not cope with such variety. Until the early twentieth century, canning on the Columbia remained a labor-intensive operation with much hand manufacture, soldering, venting, and resealing.

The changes brought by steam in the 1860s and 1870s can seem trivial when compared to the older energy cycles of the Columbia. In the decades following the opening of the first cannery on the Columbia in 1866, salmon still swam against the river's current and human labor still secured fish. The canneries preserved fish as Indians had preserved fish, through the application of heat—that is, energy. Where Indians used the sun or a wood fire to dry fish, the canneries used steam to cook and to can them. The preservation of salmon still meant that fish could be consumed by people who neither fished nor lived on the Columbia.

But pull back a little, widen your vision, and the changes become apparent. Canneries had helped organize an old set of tasks in a profoundly new way. Even partially mechanized canneries so greatly increased the scale of everything—time, space, organization, and energy—as to make the Indian harvest seem distant and unrecognizable. Whereas harvest, manufacture, and transport by the Indians had remained largely nonmechanical and used only small increments of energy, the canneries (despite their limits) depended on steam engines for manufacture and transport. Whereas most salmon preserved by Indians usually lasted no more than six months, canned salmon lasted for many years. Whereas the Indian trade in preserved fish remained within the region, the canneries shipped fish around the world. Whereas the labor of producing dried salmon depended largely on the cooperative labor of Indian kin groups, the canneries organized hundreds of workers related to each other largely by their work itself and created new tasks for them.

In 1889, Rudyard Kipling, traveling as a journalist and tourist, was a passenger on a Columbia River steamer that stopped at a fish wheel to pick up a night's catch of salmon. Kipling gave the machines that mediated late-nineteenth-century human relations with the Columbia an emblematic significance, and the fish wheel was a remarkable machine. Turning in the current of the river, its buckets scooped out "salmon by the hundred—huge fifty pounders, hardly dead, scores of twenty and thirty pounders, and a host of smaller fish. They were all Chenook [sic] salmon . . . That is to say they were royal salmon." Humans built the fish wheels, adjusted them, and tended them, but the harvest itself was automatic and impersonal. Except when a giant sturgeon jammed the machine and its smashed and torn body had to be removed manually, the slaughter was purely mechanical.

Taken by one machine, the salmon were carried by another, the steamer, to a cannery: "a crazy building . . . quivering with the machinery on its floors." Kipling watched Chinese workers, "blood-besmeared yellow devils," cut and package flesh. He was "impressed not so much with the speed of the manufacture as the character of the factory. Inside, on a floor ninety by forty, the most civilized and murderous of machinery. Outside, three footsteps, the thick growing pines and the immense solitude of the hills."

For Kipling the canneries encapsulated a basic spatial division between the mechanical and the natural. Inside, crowding, humanity, death, machines, routinization; outside, solitude, nature, life, the organic, and freedom. He asserted a temporal division. Mechanization was the mark of the modern; nature was a primordial past. He displaced onto the Chinese his own unease with the mechanical order that was mutilating the "Royal Chenook" and the whole organic Columbia. In Kipling there is regret at the mechanization of the organic and a common racist demonology—the Chinese are "blood-besmeared yellow devils"; they are slaves to machines and their degradation is all the more striking because unspoiled nature lies just beyond the door.

What disturbed Kipling was the loss of a direct contact with nature. The whole trajectory of his travel sketch is backward, away from the "progress" represented by the fish wheel and the cannery. Kipling felt a need to restore a more organic relation, to capture the salmon by matching his own power against theirs. He went fishing with rod and reel.

Kipling restored a proper masculine relation with nature as a direct contest with living things. He fished to reestablish a connection unmediated by machines. But his resolution was unintentionally ironic. Kipling fished the Clackamas, a tributary of the Willamette, near where a weir kept the salmon and steelhead from moving upstream to spawn. The weir was for a hatchery; it capitalized on and thwarted the instinct that brought the salmon home. The elaborate rituals that joined salmon egg and sperm yielded to knives cutting flesh and eggs and sperm meeting in metal containers.

Kipling's version of the river in which the machine alienated human labor from nature was hardly original. Similar readings would contribute to the American cult of the wilderness, to national parks, to maintaining manhood through sport. Kipling offered a predictable and privileged primitivism as an antidote to alienation. Factories and cities took humans away from nature; leisure brought them back.

For all its unarguable influence, however, Kipling's view was not necessarily the dominant American view, and it certainly can't explain the half century of the Columbia's history that followed his visit. The actual world could not be bifurcated so cleanly. Kipling rode on steamships to criticize steam's power to alienate. He returned to nature at a hatchery. He caught fish whose destiny was as tied to the new industrial order as was the fate of those that entered the cannery.

Something more tangled, more complicated, and more paradoxical was going on. When they talked about the Columbia, when they talked about nature, Americans might duplicate Kipling's dichotomies, but when they acted on the river Americans were Emersonians.

Emerson was American capitalism's poet/philosopher. He provided an amazingly facile and flexible reading of a natural world in which both a Rudyard Kipling and a cannery owner could find comfort, inspiration, and justification. For Emerson, nature mattered because natural facts were expressions of enduring spiritual facts. A river's flux expressed the flux of life itself. Nature made beauty and spirit accessible to human reason, a Kantian Reason which intuitively and spontaneously grasped larger patterns.

Kantian Reason perceived the beauty and order of nature, but Kantian Understanding grasped its utility. Understanding transformed nature into the machine. Nature did not object to such manipulation. It happily consented. "Nature is thoroughly mediate. It is made to serve. It receives the dominion of man as meekly as the ass on which the Saviour rode." Nature educated its students in the "doctrine of Use, namely, that a thing is good only so far as it serves." The mechanical was not the antithesis of nature, but its realization in a new form. Steam was wind in the boiler of the boat, trains imitated eagles or swallows darting from town to town. What seemed ugly in isolation became beauty when reattached to "the Whole."

In thinking of themselves both as children of nature (nature's nation) and as children of the machine (masters of American know-how) Americans were Emersonians. Emerson reconciled nature with the busy, manipulative world of American capitalism. He reconciled utilitarianism with idealism; he reconciled the practical and the spiritual. When humans acted on nature they did not defile it, they purified it. "Art was nature passed through the alembic of man."

Emerson could simultaneously rejoice in the ability of the machine to subjugate and control nature and in the spiritual truth and inspiration nature provided. Kipling fled the machine; Emerson, in Leo Marx's words, found the industrial revolution "a railway journey in the direction of nature." In Emersonian terms, putting land or water to work was opening, at least potentially, a new access to nature. Emerson had rejoiced in the "magic" of railroad iron, "its power to evoke the sleeping energies of land and water." Every American, he also proclaimed, "should be educated with a view to the values of the land." The "nervous, rocky West" would be transformed into a garden, and its people, "grown up in the bowers of a paradise," would transform the nation.

What by and large fell out of this Emersonian version of nature was work. Emerson recognized that in their striving the new American capitalists actually disdained labor. Americans were, Emerson wrote in 1847,

> an ardent race, and are as fully possessed with that hatred of labor, which is the principle of progress in the human race, as any other people. They must and will have enjoyment without the sweat. So they buy slaves, where the women will permit, where they will not, they make the wind, the tide, the waterfall, the steam, the cloud, the lightning do the work, by every art and device their cunningest brain can achieve.

Capitalism could easily embrace an Emersonianism in which the machine put nature to work and reduced human labor.

As the Oregon Steam Navigation Company discovered, nature and machines in proper combination provided the opportunity for immense wealth and power. On the Columbia the key was converting the portages to private property. John Ainsworth and his partners in the Oregon Steam Navigation Company controlled the river's south bank at the

Dalles and the Cascades. They replaced human porters with animals, and eventually animals with steam. They built twenty miles of portage railroad that in 1880 linked the company's twenty-six steamboats. Until the coming of the transcontinental railroads, the company moved virtually everything and everybody that went up and down the river.

Portland and the Oregon Steam Navigation Company prospered together. Political boundaries that divided the region into the state of Oregon and the territories of Washington and Idaho had little impact on the networks of economic power. The mines of Idaho and the wheat of Washington belonged to Portland. The Oregon Steam Navigation Company made Portland the region's commercial heart and the Columbia its artery.

But the Oregon Steam Navigation Company's combination of nature's energy and mechanical energy was tenuous. The company thrived in the predatory world of nineteenth-century capitalism because it operated in a backwater so distant from the East and California as not to excite the attention of more powerful rivals.

In 1874 such a rival eventually appeared in the person of Henry Villard. Villard, a cultured German immigrant and journalist, came to rescue the investments of German bondholders in the failing enterprises of Ben Holliday, a decidedly uncultured stagecoach entrepreneur who, seeing the future, had moved from animal power to steam power by investing in Oregon railroads and steamship lines. Villard took control of Holliday's enterprises, bought out the OSNC (at a price of $3,320,000), reorganized it as the Oregon Railway and Navigation Company (ORNC), teamed it with the Northern Pacific, and linked the Pacific Northwest to the East by rail.

During the 1880s the Northern Pacific freed transportation from the water but not from the river. The river acted as the railroad's grading crew, cutting through the Cascades. For a while the Columbia would still determine how goods moved east and west. But when the Northern Pacific built its main line to its terminus in Tacoma on Puget Sound, and as other railroads—the Union Pacific, the Great Northern, the Milwaukee Road—arrived in the region, the Columbia lost its primacy in linking the lands west and east of the Cascade Mountains.

Both Portland merchants and interior farmers lamented the loss. The merchants saw wheat that once came to them go to Tacoma and Seattle. The farmers believed the railroads overcharged them, and river transportation could force freight rates down. The federal government had subsidized the Northern Pacific, and now farmers and merchants turned, as Westerners have always done in such situations, to the federal government.

Oregonians sought to transform the river—to tame the bar, deepen channels, and blast passages through rapids. To change the river, they needed the U.S. Army Corps of Engineers. The Corps worked both upstream and downstream from Portland. They were most successful downstream. By the early twentieth century huge jetties directed the river's energy to carve a stable channel over the bar at the Columbia's mouth. Dikes and dredging progressively deepened a channel in the river so large that ocean vessels could reach Portland. Humans forced the river to remove part of the sands and silt it annually deposited, and they took the rest, filling in marshes and creating new land.

The Corps failed to create such a "free river" upstream. The locks at the Cascades did not open until 1896, nearly a quarter of a century after the first survey. The federal government opened a canal at the Dalles in 1915. Like the Cascade locks, it was an impressive technical achievement. But neither canal ever carried much freight. Between 1896 and 1923 the Cascades canal moved only 29,500 tons annually. The canals were guns aimed at the railroads, and the railroads responded by lowering their rates, but the guns lacked firepower. Lower railroad rates drove the steamboats out of business. Once symbols of power, the steamers gradually became obsolete, the stuff of nostalgic memory. Regular boat service through the Dalles-Celilo canal ended in 1917. Regular service between Portland and the Dalles ceased in 1923. It was a losing business. Between 1928 and 1933 no traffic at all moved through the canal. The costly works went unused.

Steamboats, railroads, and locks mediated between humans and the river, but this new technology masked its ties to both nature and human labor. One had to look closely to see that Emerson was right, that steamboats and railroads were not the antithesis of nature. When compared to the flowing river, the clanging, hissing, smoking steam engine seemed resolutely unnatural. There was nature in a steam engine's bowels, but it was far less obvious than the stunning nature of the Columbia Gorge that could be seen from the windows of steamboats and Pullman cars. Steam engines consumed nature. They burned Kipling's "pines" to produce their steam. The *Bailey Gatzert*, one of the majestic steamers of the White Collar Line, burned "three cords of pitchy slabwood" each hour to power a 1,300-horsepower engine. The wood growing along the banks of the river fueled the steamers' ascent. The country east of the Dalles, however, was unforested. And so when strong winds blew from the west up the Columbia Gorge, wood barges hoisted sail carrying cargoes of cordwood for distribution at the Dalles to steamboats operating upstream. The organic—wind and wood— necessarily supported the mechanical.

Railroads, fouling the air with cinders and smoke, burned not modern trees but ancient vegetation. They took coal, a fossil fuel, stored energy captured by plants from the sun millions of years before, and used it to carry loads the river had once carried. A locomotive's tie with nature seemed even more tenuous than a steamboat's.

Steamboats and locomotives masked human labor quite as thoroughly as they masked nature. Humans no longer rowed, towed, and hauled their way upriver; sweat and aching muscles remained, but they vanished belowdecks with the boiler crew. Labor became obvious only at the points where nature was becoming machine or when nature halted the progress of machines. Labor built the machines and loaded the wood the steamboats burned. Labor reappeared at the Cascades and the Dalles and Portland, where rapids or the end of tidewater required that cargo be unloaded and reloaded. Here humans lifted, carried and dragged. In this world of steam and white water it was human labor that sutured together the steam engines on the water and the steam engines on the rail.

But the same machines that masked labor also created new opportunities for labor. Development along the Columbia brought in workers from all over the world: Chinese, Norwegians, Italians, Finns, and others. Steam engines and canneries enabled workers to can salmon and to carry the cans outward to a world as wide as the one from which they had come.

This new work depended on precise organization of humans and nature, and this organization was spatial. In this new world of work, race divided space. White fishermen denied the river to the Chinese, whose competition they feared. The Chinese space was largely inside, only the dead salmon spilling in by the thousands linked them to the river. Hired for a season by labor contractors, more than 4,000 Chinese worked in thirty-five Columbia River canneries in 1881. They lived in bunkhouses at the more isolated canneries; they were clustered in boardinghouses along two blocks of Bond Street in Astoria. In Astoria, when the salmon runs thickened in the river and the boats came in heavy with fish, the Chinese were awakened at 4 a.m. and set to work.

Indians, too, came to know racialized space. In the Northwest reservations were never as confining as elsewhere. Many Indians never moved to them at all but instead remained along the Columbia. The treaties they had signed promised them the right to fish at their usual and accustomed places. But many whites regarded Indians and treaties as archaic nuisances. Particularly at the Dalles and Celilo Falls, they shoved the Indians aside when they could, commandeering some of their best fishing sites for fish wheels. Indians who had once organized the space of the entire river now fought for independent access to a much narrowed space.

But the racialization of the river's space was only the crudest of divisions. Gender and class also subdivided the river. The Chinese Exclusion Act of 1882 left a shrinking and aging Chinese workforce. At Astoria they were replaced by Finnish and Norwegian women, the wives and daughters of fishermen, who inherited the confined interior space of the Chinese. They, in turn, would yield part of this space to Filipino, Mexican, and Japanese workers.

Out of doors, class as well as race divided the river. Kipling, in retreating to a rod and reel, took his salmon on the Willamette. In selecting how and where he fished, he gave away his class. How and where men caught fish reflected a class struggle.

A failure to recognize how the river was socially marked and controlled can lead to basic mistakes. Too often, economic models in which the social and historical hardly figure at all have been relied on to explain declining fisheries. The fisheries are a commons, this argument goes; the problem they faced was one of human nature. Each fisherman seeks to maximize his return; each seeks more efficient ways to compete. No one has an incentive to maintain stocks, for they have no guarantee that others will not reap the benefits.

This is what Garrett Hardin referred to as the tragedy of the commons: the inevitable tendency of consumers of a common resource to overexploit it. But historians know that Hardin's model of the commons is an invention. No such simple commons has ever operated. It never existed on the Columbia. In historical practice users of common resources set up rules and limits; they created customs; they limited access. Fishermen made the actual Columbia a complicated patchwork of competing claims and practices. Indians possessed treaty rights. Gillnetters controlled access to particular drifts: stretches of the river where they cast their nets and floated downstream. Fixed-gear men with their pound nets commandeered space on the river. Their very equipment fenced out others. Fish wheels took over old Indian fishing sites and pushed aside the Indians, despite the treaty rights which promised them a particular share of the commons.

Gillnetters were at the center of the struggle for the river commons because they were the largest group of fishermen. In the nineteenth century the canneries rented boats and nets to immigrants accustomed to the water. The counts were never exact, but there were at least 1,700 gillnetters in 1883, with the number dipping to a low of 1,224 in 1890. The number peaked at 2,596 in 1904.

In the late nineteenth century the mosquito fleet (as the boats of the gillnetters were called) covered the river below Portland from May to August. Their nets formed a vast floating barrier to salmon—545 miles long by the late 1880s if connected and stretched end to end—but the daily catch of any individual boat was small. In 1891 and 1892, George and Barker, one of the Astoria canneries, kept track of the gillnetters' average daily catch. Early in the runs the boats averaged only three fish a day. When the runs grew stronger at the end of May and early June and again in July, the boats might average ten to twelve fish. At the peak of the run, they brought in eighteen or twenty fish a day. During the heyday of the runs, the aggregate of these catches was more than the canneries could handle. In the early twentieth century the canneries had to institute limits of 800 pounds per boat for several days around the Fourth of July. Anything above that was waste. Twenty fish could amount to more than 800 pounds, since among them were the big spring chinooks, locally called hogs. These fish ran fifty or sixty pounds or more. Kipling saw them. We never will. They no longer exist.

Although they operated in a world of steam, gillnetters continued to rely on wind and human muscle to harvest fish. A distinctive Columbia River fishing vessel evolved in the Astoria boatyards. The vessels were small (twenty-five feet long), single-masted, and equipped with oars. They were open, only partially decked, and took two men, the captain and the puller, to sail and operate. The men could rig the sail as a tent and sleep under it.

To catch fish the gillnetters had to control a three-dimensional space which extended across and beneath the surface of the river. This space was a drift—a two- to five-mile section of the river through which the tide pulled the boat and its net. All gill nets work on a simple principle: fish swim into them but cannot fit through their mesh. In trying to extricate themselves, they get caught by the gills and drown. The art of gillnetting involved disguising the net so fish could neither see it nor avoid it. Thus gillnetters fished at night or when the river was muddy. They altered the design of the nets to keep fish from swimming underneath them or above them. By introducing layers of different-size mesh, they could take both large and small fish, enmeshing the big ones, catching the small ones by the gills. Their nets and their methods of using them embodied a working knowledge of nature.

But gillnetters modified as well as knew nature and the river. Floating nets dominated the river from Point Ellice to the mouth, but above Tongue Point by 1900 gillnetters turned to diver nets. The cork line at the top of the diver net was just buoyant enough to keep the net vertical in the river while the lead line sank down to touch bottom. The gillnetters could not use the net where the bottom was littered with snags or debris, for they would tear the net. They needed to clear the bottom, and to do so the fishermen on particular drifts created snag unions. By virtue of their labor, members of a snag union claimed exclusive fishing rights on that drift.

To watch gillnetters at work was to witness an elaborately choreographed dance of fish, river, and men. The habits of fish, the hydraulics of the river, and the organized labor of men all intersected. Labor and nature merged. No element, no movement could be separated from the other; each, to some degree, shaped the other. On a summer's dawn with the sails against the blue sky and green forest, with the fish silver in the net, the result was a thing of brutal beauty. When the canneries had disappeared, when the fishing fleet on the Columbia had shrunk nearly to the vanishing point, when Astoria lived on memories of fish, what stuck in human memories were flashes of color, of movement, of bodies, both fish and human, that seemed too vivid and elemental to have been so transitory. Edward Beard, who rose to become a partner in a cannery, could at the end of his life remember no more beautiful sight than the mosquito fleet sailing out of Astoria on a Sunday evening against the setting sun.

But the beauty was brutal because fish died in astonishing numbers and because men died in chilling numbers. Cleaning the river's bottom, dividing and allocating its space did not domesticate the river. Gill-netting was dangerous; its practitioners "hardy and brave." There was a constant temptation to prolong the net's drift, but if the fishing boat came too close to the bar, its breakers could ensnare both nets and boat. In the 1880s an estimated twenty to sixty fishermen died annually on the Columbia bar. And when storms surprised the fleet, as the gale of May 7, 1880, did, the toll was terrible. That storm hit the fleet with many boats drifting, "hanging on their nets," as the gillnetters said. Desperately, the fishermen cut their nets and fled. The winds capsized some, and ripped apart the sails of others, driving them onto Chinook Point. Even many who reached their anchorages foundered there. The storm claimed eighty boats and forty-five fishermen.

But gillnetters also died because they competed against other fish-ermen for space on the river. The Columbia fishery was not a homo-geneous space. Fish were much more reliably found in some areas than others, and mechanical devices secured those areas for particular own-ers. Fish traps—originally wooden traps of piles and slats—grew with the canning industry, but by 1890 they had yielded to more sophisticated and expensive pound nets introduced by fishermen from the Great Lakes. Steam pile drivers drove in permanent piles to which nets were attached that extended out from the riverbank. Salmon meeting the barrier followed it away from the shore to a heart-shaped container which, in turn, steered them into smaller webbed areas, first a "pot," then a "spiller," from which they were removed. By 1889 there were 121 traps in Baker Bay alone. In all, there were nearly 400 fish traps and pound nets in operation. Gillnetters who tried to fish the bay risked snaring their own nets on the traps and endangering their own lives.

By the turn of the century the chinooks that escaped the gill nets and pound nets had also to evade seine nets operated from shore before facing more than forty fish wheels between the Cascades and Celilo Falls. These devices, either fixed on shore or mounted on scows with artificial leads to guide fish, first appeared on the Columbia in 1879 at the same sites prized by Indian dipnetters where the water was swift

and the fish in their migration upstream were forced into narrow channels. Fish wheels never took more than 7 percent of the total catch,
but their efficiency, as Major W. A. Jones reported to the U.S. Fisheries
Commission in 1887, was "painful." They literally pumped fish out of ✓
the river. During the height of the runs their individual output was
tremendous, with each taking an average of 20,000 pounds of fish a
day. The record, set in the 1880s, was 50,000 pounds in a day.

By the early twentieth century there were not enough salmon for all
who sought them. The runs of spring and summer chinook had been
visibly declining since the 1880s. Major Jones noted that between April
and August it was "a sort of a miracle that any fish escape to go up the
river, except the small Blue backs, Steelheads, and the precocious St.
Jacob's Chinook which can pass through the 4½ inch mesh of the
gillnets." By 1890 salmon were growing scarce at the Indian fishery of
Kettle Falls. On the Yakima, overfishing weakened the runs; irrigation
depleted the river and nearly killed them. Based on anecdotal evidence,
there had been a dramatic decline in the runs of chinook on the Snake
and its tributaries by the 1890s.

Preserving salmon was, however, as much a social and cultural matter
as a biological or economic one. On the river humans struggled to turn
space into property and salmon into a commodity, but this was only
part of the transformation of nature taking place. In their dying, salmon
revealed constellations of competing social values. Understanding the *and*
fate of salmon involves understanding complicated and particular social *econ,*
struggles and not some universal human nature at work in an undif- *systems*
ferentiated commons. *??*

Gillnetters most fully elaborated the cultural and social meaning of
fishing. They did so through the Columbia River Fishermen's Protective
Union. Not much survives of the early union. There is a ledger—
fittingly enough, water-soaked. The ink on many of its pages that record
the minutes of meetings, the payments of dues, the greetings to other
unions is runny and blurred. Sofus Jensen, the union secretary, pains-
takingly wrote those now blurred pages, and what remains clear is his
working-class disdain for the canners and all he regarded as their lackeys.

When Jensen wrote, the union was already a decade old. It faced a
formidable foe. In the early years of the fishery the canners owned the
boats and nets that the fishermen rented; they were also the only market
for the gillnetters' catch. In 1886, despite a declining catch, the canners

had cut the price they offered for salmon. The fishermen had successfully struck for higher prices and subsequently secured collective bargaining for the price they would receive for salmon. In this they merely imitated the canners, who had long set, and held, a standard opening price.

The dangers of their work, the decline of the salmon, and their exploitation by the canneries sharpened the animosities of the gillnetters. They thought of themselves as craftsmen whose tools were boat and net; their relation to the canners was that of workers to bosses, of labor to capital.

The gillnetters, however, never portrayed themselves solely as immigrant laborers resisting capitalist bosses, for to do so would be to play into the hands of their enemies. In 1880 six of every seven fishermen in Clatsop County were foreign-born, and most were transients who arrived with the salmon and departed when the runs ended. In the off-season they logged, mined, or sought other seasonal labor. As transient immigrant laborers, the gillnetters were vulnerable to attack as outsiders plundering the river of its resources. They compared poorly to the pound-net men and fish-wheel owners, who were, as an 1887 report to the Oregon legislature put it, more likely to be "riparian owners; . . . resident citizens and taxpayers."

Through their union, the gillnetters rhetorically turned the tables on their opponents. They forged an identity as American workers whose labor naturalized them in the dual sense of the word. They were farmers of both the sea and the land. They worked the river during fishing season and, they claimed, their farms the rest of the year. Both as workers and as "farmers," the gillnetters created an identity rooted in a nature they knew through work. They knew nature's power, for they risked life and property. They lay out on "stormy waters night and day," suffering hardships. On the other hand, they knew nature's beneficence, for they worked the "ocean farm," where they could reap without planting. From nature's bounty and the strength of their union, gillnetters claimed they created families, stability, and moral order.

Gillnetters denounced their opponents, both canners and fixed-gear men, as capitalists who ruined and degraded both labor and nature. Capitalists perverted work by using machines to plunder nature and displace human labor. Gillnetters deployed this rhetoric to try to gain privileged access to the fishery. They had the wit to recognize that fishing, like any human relation with nature, is as much social and ideological as it is biological. Crises in the Columbia fishery have never been just questions of salmon; they have been questions of proper ways of life.

The major struggle for privileged access to the fishery matched gill-netters against those who fished with fixed gear. It went on from the late nineteenth century until the 1930s. The gillnetters sought to persuade the federal government and the states of Oregon and Washington to exclude pound nets and fish wheels from the river. Fixed-gear men sought to restrict gillnetting and bar foreigners from the fishery. Although each side claimed it sought to protect the salmon runs, the actual debate had more to do with the social consequences of each kind of fishing and the social identity of the fishermen.

In a developing capitalist country, the fixed-gear men seemed to hold all the cards. Pound nets and fish wheels, owned by native-born Americans, delivered fresher and less bruised fish to the canneries at a lower cost and with less risk of human life. Because they simply confined the fish in the nets, pound-net men could better regulate their catch and thus more easily conserve and protect the runs.

Gillnetters tried to counter by attacking pound-net men for taking small, and they thought immature, salmon that escaped the gill nets. The gillnetters cited a theory, one that had currency into the early twentieth century, that all salmon did not die while spawning; some went back to the sea to return again. But such arguments turned out to be specious. Taking small salmon as well as large made little difference if *all* salmon proceeding upriver spawned and died.

Dealt such a weak biological and economic hand, the gillnetters seized the social and moral high ground. Against the market economy gillnetters appealed to a moral economy. They made the high yields of fixed gear a weakness. Fish traps "annihilated" salmon for the profit of "moneyed individuals" who "could take their gold and go elsewhere."

What did it matter if a great food producing industry was destroyed solely for private gain, so long as few made fortunes and the fisherman and laborer starved amidst plenty? Capital, you know, must be protected.

Fish traps and fish wheels demanded much capital and little labor. The salmon disappeared and labor suffered, and a country "supposed to be run on the plan of 'the greatest good to the greatest number,' " served forty or fifty individuals instead of "the toiling thousands." How human beings labored on the river, how the proceeds were distributed, mattered more than the total yield of their labor.

For many years the result of this ideological battle was a standoff. Sometimes the results were laughable. In 1908 the gillnetters and fish-wheel operators sponsored competing initiatives which were placed before Oregon voters. The gillnetters proposed closing the upper Columbia to all gear but hook and line, thus eliminating seines and fish wheels. The fixed-gear men proposed restricting fishing to daylight hours, effectively abolishing gillnetting. Gillnetters claimed fish-wheel operators were destroying the runs; fish-wheel operators blamed gillnetters for the decline of the fisheries. Oregon voters believed both of them; they passed both initiatives. But because Oregon shared the river with Washington, gillnetters simply got licenses in Washington, efforts at enforcement failed, and subsequent legislation in effect repealed the laws.

Such regulatory fiascos were the rule. The gillnetters never secured federal intervention, and early attempts at state regulation proved largely ineffective because of competing jurisdictions and lack of serious enforcement. Heavy fishing pressure and logging and grazing that damaged spawning habitat upstream ensured the continued decline of the runs. The canneries adapted to the shortage of spring and summer chinook by extending the fishery into September and taking fall chinook. They added sockeye and steelhead to the pack, and then silvers. Eventually they even packed chum salmon.

The introduction of small gasoline-powered vessels and a growing market for cold storage (or mild cured) salmon extended the fishing season both temporally and spatially. When the salmon were not running or when state regulations halted fishing in the river, the gasoline-powered gillnetting vessels went out beyond the bar after them. They now doubled as trollers, fishing with hook and line. Fishermen took large chinooks in the ocean before they returned to spawn. The total catch increased, peaked in 1911, fluctuated for a while, and then began an inexorable decline after 1925.

The decline of the natural runs gave force to claims that humans needed to intervene in the spawning process itself to create more fish.

Hatcheries sought to wed technology and biology, to merge factorylike production with natural reproduction. The canners, many fishermen, and many experts on the fisheries came to regard nature as inefficient. H. A. Jones, the federal official who first studied the decline of the Columbia fisheries, produced a rather typical piece of nineteenth-century arithmetic. He calculated that a $10,000 investment in a single hatchery and operating expenses of $3,000 a year would produce 5 million mature fish a year, which, when canned, would yield $5 million. This was more than twice the fish and twice the income then being produced on the Columbia. "These figures border on the marvelous," Jones admitted, but encapsulated in such marvelous numbers was a hope that an inefficient nature, with a helping managerial hand, could solve both a biological and a social crisis.

The new hatcheries that proliferated in the early twentieth century operated uninhibited by any actual knowledge of the life cycle of salmon. By 1920 it had become apparent, as one Bureau of Fisheries study put it, that "the hatcheries probably inflicted as much, or more, damage to the salmon runs than they had service of value."

By then the fishery was taking on an almost Frankensteinian form. Humans had begun to turn something natural into something monstrous. For thousands of years Indian peoples had recognized and understood the blessings of a world in which small fish left the river, harvested the greater solar energy available in the ocean, and returned as very big fish. These fish always returned at the same time to the same place, and in their return they followed paths which took them to spots where human labor secured their capture. Indians knew these places and had developed techniques that allowed them to expend less energy on capturing fish than the whites who followed. The salmon that escaped the nets and spears returned to their spawning grounds, which yielded new runs in subsequent years. White gillnetters, as much as Indians, could only regard such an arrangement as providential. A "greater One than we has done all the planting," and fishermen had "only to reap." It was as if seed wheat left home in April to return as a field of grain in September. It was as if deer came walking through town every November.

And in the face of such regularity and bounty, the Americans began breeding the fish in factories and setting out to sea to catch them. Each step of the process that led to this result was logical. It was only the result that was mad. Like many kinds of madness, this one looked quite sane from the inside. One thing followed quite understandably from another until both a kind of environmental insanity and a bitter social conflict were achieved.

Emerson's railway back to nature seemed to have been derailed, but it was a journey that most Americans were not willing to forsake. Emersonianism took a powerful new form in the early twentieth century. Boosters like Rufus Woods, engineers like Willis Batcheller and James O'Sullivan, intellectuals like Lewis Mumford, politicians like Gifford Pinchot and Franklin Delano Roosevelt, radicals like Woody Guthrie: all would be Emersonian when they looked at the river.

II

Emerson's vision of the machine as a force of nature found its fullest expression as part of the old romance of energy in Western society, a dream of liberation from labor, an end to social conflict and environmental degradation through the harnessing of nature's power to human purposes. As much as the gillnetters' contest for salmon, these dreams of energy involved the river as a scene of social struggle. Rarely has the hope of transformation through energy shimmered more brightly or been fought for more ardently than along the Columbia River in the 1920s and 1930s. Today, with the Columbia dammed, those dreams seem collective self-deceptions. But we have really not so much given up our energy dreams as transferred them to other sources: to solar power or to nuclear fusion, clean and unlimited energy that will supposedly save us and our world yet. The dams on the Columbia are no longer an object of romance; they have become a necessary evil. The original passion is, however, worth understanding.

In the 1920s the energy of the Columbia River still remained largely untapped. In July 1880, Henry Villard, then in the process of turning the Oregon Steam Navigation Company into the Oregon Railway and Navigation Company, outfitted the company's new steamer (yet another *Columbia*) with incandescent lamps. When the *Columbia* docked in Portland, the crew ran wires from the vessel to the Clarendon Hotel and suspended lights over First Street, which was "lighted up . . . to the brightness of day." Thousands visited "the light and the vessel."

But it would be more than a half century before electricity from the Columbia, the river, rather than the *Columbia*, the steamship, illuminated Portland.

During that half century electricity demonstrated its potential for reconfiguring the space of Portland and its hinterland. It powered trolleys and interurbans that changed where people lived and the relation between residential space and workplace. Part of this electricity came from the Columbia's tributaries at Willamette Falls and, later, at the headwaters of the Clackamas.

Tapping the energy of flowing water was not new, but the ability to use that power far from a river's shore was new and startling. Waterwheels and then turbines had long turned the motion of water into the motion of shafts, gears, and belts that transferred energy to the whirring, turning machines humans used to cut, grind, hammer, shape, and spin. But to use the power of the river, one had to be close enough to spit in it. Waterfalls and rapids determined where energy could be used and climate determined when it was available. When streamflow declined, so did available power.

Electricity itself did not alter this equation between location and use. Both steam and water could turn turbines, and so both could produce electricity. Because direct electrical current could not be transmitted efficiently, however, steam initially possessed the advantage. Steam plants could be built near sites of consumption, but hydroelectricity remained tied to the river. Alternating current changed this; all electricity could be transmitted and consumed miles from where it was produced.

Given its wealth of mountain rivers and its relative paucity of coal, the Pacific Northwest understandably turned to hydroelectricity more extensively than other sections of the country. As early as 1889 the Willamette Falls Electric Company, one of the eventual components of Portland General Electric, successfully transmitted electricity through a fourteen-mile-long transmission line (then the longest in the country) from Willamette Falls to Portland. And although the utility always maintained a mix of steam plants (which burned "hog fuel" made from wood waste) and hydroelectric plants, the bulk of its power came from tributaries of the Columbia.

But, except for a small plant at Priest Rapids, power still did not come from the Columbia itself. The problems were not technical; they were financial. By 1925, in the words of one engineer, the hydraulic turbine had become "one of the most marvelous machines ever fabricated by the hand of man." It extracted 94 percent of the power "of a great falling current of water in the short space of 3 to 5 feet of travel through its runners within less than one-tenth of a second of time." In a small space and a flash of time turbines picked the pockets of falling water and turned the stolen energy into electricity. But building turbines and the dams and reservoirs necessary to make them work demanded huge amounts of capital.

And growing technical capacity only created new problems. Dams on the Columbia could generate far more power than the region needed or demanded. Before World War I utilities sold most of their power in cities for street and home lighting and to traction companies to run electric trolleys and the interurbans. Demand steadily increased, but not on a scale that justified damming the Columbia. When the Oregon State Engineer in 1912 explored the possibility of a dam at the Dalles, he found the dam would produce enough power to supply a city thirteen times the size of Portland. But there was no city thirteen times the size of Portland to buy it, and Portland General Electric already supplied Portland. And so the engineer imagined an industrial market: a new nitrate factory that absorbed most of the power, steel mills, and electrochemical industries.

But most industries did not buy electricity from central stations. Factories remained self-contained. They burned coal to heat their buildings and generate power. In the Northwest lumbermills burned their own wood waste, ran their own generators, and had excess power to sell.

World War I changed all this. The war bared the weakness of the existing energy system. Instead of moving electricity—"energy freed from substance," energy with no "material expression"—the United States moved mountains of coal. Moving coal to where it was consumed demanded one-third of the total carrying capacity of the railroads. And with mobilization for the war, the demands for coal increased even as the transportation system had to transport men and equipment to eastern ports for embarkation to Europe. The nation lacked sufficient coal cars, and those the railroads possessed became snarled in massive traffic jams in the eastern ports. In 1917–18 the worst winter storms in half a century

froze the jammed rail system into icy gridlock. Coal ceased to move, factories shut down, and people began to freeze.

In attacking the problem, the government gave utilities, which used coal more efficiently, priority in delivery. Instead of transporting coal to each factory, each with its own steam engines, it made more sense to transport the fuel to central generating stations that produced electricity to run electric motors in the factories. The war gave new impetus to conservation, to efficiency, and to production of electricity on a grand scale. To make sure that available power could be shifted to where it was needed, the government mandated tie-ins of existing transmission lines, allowing the excess production of one area to shift to another.

The new large generating stations, the interconnections between systems, the shift toward electric motors carried over into peacetime. They became, in Thomas Hughes's words, "a solution in search of a problem."

For the utilities the problem was simple: coordinating the new generating and transmission capacities in private hands and creating enough demand to use the new capacity. They called the result superpower. Superpower was an engineering scheme that advocated creating new large-scale power plants which would be integrated with existing power plants through high-voltage transmission lines. The power plants would all feed their output into a common pool which utilities would tap for distribution.

But for reformers the problem that electricity solved was industrial capitalism itself with its degradation of work and nature. What Morris L. Cooke, the Pennsylvania reformer, called Giant Power was considerably more ambitious. Its "immediate objective" was "the conversion of all our primary energy resources into electricity and their pooling into regional systems which will then be integrated into a nationwide federation of systems." Reorganizing energy production was but a means to reorganize society; social engineering would allow increased power production "to effect immeasurably for good the lives of all the people." Giant Power would bring electricity to rural areas that still lacked it. It was a plan "by which most of the drudgery of human life can be taken from the shoulders of men and women who toil, and replaced by the power of electricity."

Gifford Pinchot brought to Giant Power the same moral zeal that

he had brought to forestry. As governor of Pennsylvania, he was convinced that regional integration and its social benefits were possible only under public control. He enlisted Morris L. Cooke in a campaign to make Giant Power a reality. Electricity was so powerful, Pinchot declared, that "[e]ither we must control electric power, or its masters and owners will control us." Initially, the government would regulate utilities; eventually, it would probably own them. The utilities predictably denounced Giant Power as socialism. Pinchot predictably denounced his opponents as selfish, avaricious monopolists.

Pinchot tried and failed to achieve Giant Power in Pennsylvania. Superpower—the consolidation and integration of existing facilities—went forward; it took the form of holding companies and capitalists held the reins. But on the Columbia something close to Giant Power stirred. Public ownership, rural electrification, generating facilities far from the source of consumption—that is, the eradication of distance as a significant factor in energy development—were all marks of Giant Power; they were also eventually the characteristics of development on the Columbia.

Rufus Woods, the editor of the *Wenatchee Daily World*, was no Gifford Pinchot. In the 1920s he saw public utilities as leading to the "vortex of state socialism." He unsuccessfully opposed Washington's public-power initiative in 1930.

Rufus Woods was a western booster in the grand tradition. He was at heart a showman—one summer he toured with the Cole Bros. Circus as a clown. "Play it big," he would tell his staff. "Play it like a circus." He knew what would play in the small towns of the Columbia Basin. Woods might oppose public power in principle, but he ardently supported big government dams on the Columbia if they provided capital and growth for Wenatchee. What Woods boosted above all was the Grand Coulee Dam. Willis Batcheller, a Seattle engineer, was the first to prove the dam technically feasible. James O'Sullivan, a lawyer and engineer and a consistent advocate of public power, was the dam's theorist and its most ardent promoter. Arguing that the dam's power production could finance its irrigation operations, he vigorously lobbied for its construction.

But it was Woods who had the genius to cast the battle for the Grand Coulee Dam as a melodrama. His paper published a commemorative issue whose boxed subtitle told it all:

How there was used a Gigantic Hoax—
POLITICS—INTRIGUE—MISINFORMATION—THREATS—
DECEIT—BIG MONEY—RIDICULE—INTIMIDATION—
to obstruct the World's Greatest Power and Irrigation Project—
and HOW THEY ALL FAILED!

From years of lobbying, Chamber of Commerce politics, dull and dreary congressional hearings, and endless studies and testimony by various government and consulting engineers, Woods created a dramatic saga full of heroes and villains. Woods and his allies had stayed true to a vision of a giant dam whose power would run pumps to lift water into the Grand Coulee. Irrigation would create homes and wealth in the desert. Woods encountered enemies at every turn: Spokane businessmen and Olympia politicians who envisioned a gravity plan for the Columbia Basin, Washington Water Power Company (a subsidiary of Electric Bond and Share), James D. Ross and Seattle City Light, the Army Corps of Engineers, Easterners in general, and midwestern farm interests in particular. He overcame them all.

Rufus Woods and his allies, especially James O'Sullivan, were formidable advocates; they were knowledgeable about the Columbia and its potential, but they were always boosters. And they knew that ultimately the fate of the Columbia would be determined in Washington, D.C.

In passing the Federal Water Power Act (1920), Congress had created the stage upon which Woods produced his drama. Because most western waterpower sites on nonnavigable rivers lay on federal lands, and because the government authority over interstate commerce gave it control over other sites on navigable rivers, the federal government could assert control over virtually all hydroelectric developments. Utility companies or municipal utilities might develop the sites, but public authorities could regulate rates and the act created the possibility of eventual federal ownership.

The immediate federal goal, however, was not Giant Power. It was the planned and balanced development of navigation, irrigation, and power on the nation's rivers. In 1926 Secretary of Commerce Herbert Hoover said that the object was the "coordinated long-view development of each river system to its maximum utilization." The Columbia drainage held 3.5 million idle horsepower, and there were 1.8 million acres in the proposed Columbia Basin Project alone awaiting irrigation. The river needed to be dammed and its flow regulated, its power tapped, and the desert made to flower.

Engineers recognized that the Columbia was the country's greatest single source of hydroelectricity, but electricity lacked committed bureaucratic sponsors. The Army Corps of Engineers regarded dams as an aid to navigation; the Bureau of Reclamation saw dams as a means of irrigation. During the 1920s reclamation and navigation were the tails that wagged the dog of power.

In the 1920s reclamation dominated discussions of the Columbia. Ironically, only the Washington Grange emphasized the benefits of power. Spokane interests battled for a gravity plan that would funnel water to the Columbia Basin from the Pend Oreille River, a tributary of the Columbia. Woods and the Wenatchee interests battled for the Grand Coulee Dam, which would produce electricity to pump water into the Grand Coulee to water the basin. Both sides agreed that reclamation came before power. The government would not finance power development except under the guise of reclaiming land or improving navigation, and neither the President nor Congress saw Columbia dams as a particularly shrewd use of large sums of public money.

Close distinctions between boondoggles and building up the country did not overly concern western boosters. Both could provide local benefits. But dams on the Columbia presented a particular challenge, for they were *neither* boondoggles *nor* clear economic progress. The very benefits they provided were their major problem. Dams would improve navigation on a river where existing navigational improvements went unused. They would bring more land into production in a country where farmers were already plagued by overproduction and low prices, and they would provide immense amounts of power which no one wanted to buy. The dams lacked economic justification.

By the late 1920s the Grand Coulee Dam seemed dead. The first step in its unlikely revival had actually come in 1925 when Congress, in House Document 308–69/1, instructed the Army Corps of Engineers to prepare plans for river basin development. Senator Wesley Jones of Washington convinced the Corps to turn a minor survey into a major study. Major John Butler did the rest. He produced the "308 Report,"

The Columbia River and Minor Tributaries, which recognized in the Columbia the potential for being the "greatest system for water power to be found anywhere in the United States." Butler imagined a Columbia eventually "controlled and managed as one system." Its immense yield of power would make the cost per unit small, although the initial investment for the ten dams the Corps envisioned would "exceed that of any other single development of any kind for power that has ever been made."

Here was Giant Power; here was heaven for boosters, but Butler quickly returned everyone to earth. There was still no economic justification. The federal government would only coordinate and approve. It left the building and financing of the dams to the states and private utilities. By 1932 only one dam, being built by Puget Sound Power and Light at Rock Island Rapids, was under construction.

In good times the 308 Report would have been only a golden nail in the coffin of Columbia development, but by the time the report came out in 1933 the country was in the midst of the Depression. The report made it clear that the Columbia's greatest resource was hydroelectric power. Faced with no actual demand for that power, advocates of the dams rediscovered electricity as a means for transforming society. The Depression provided a society desperately seeking transformation.

As with so many central ideas in American society, the utopia Americans saw shimmering in high-tension wires emerged most vividly in the work of Lewis Mumford. Mumford espoused a common energy utopianism. He made Giant Power into social theory. He thought that when we switch energy sources, we potentially change the possibilities for our society.

Mumford, in effect, explained why earlier Emersonianism had gone wrong. It had depended on the wrong energy source for its machines. Steam engines producing mechanical energy through shafts and belts belonged to what Mumford, following Patrick Geddes, called the Paleotechnic. The Paleotechnic depended on coal and iron; it represented an "upthrust into barbarism" that was hardly progress at all. It had produced a world of steady, unremitting, repetitive, monotonous toil, the toil of the canneries. Its dependence on coal had meant living on the accumulated energy capital of the past instead of on "current income." And it had wasted 90 percent of that energy. The first and defining mark of the Paleotechnic was air pollution; its by-products had yielded a "befouled and disorderly environment; the end product an exhausted one." The Paleotechnic had treated "the environment itself . . . as an abstraction. Air and sunlight because of their deplorable lack of value in exchange had no reality at all." The Paleotechnic had made abstractions into realities "whereas the realities of existence were treated . . . as abstractions, as sentimental fancies, even as aberrations . . ."

Electricity represented what Mumford called the Neotechnic. Electricity and alloys, particularly aluminum, replaced coal and iron. Hydroelectric power would purify polluted industrial cities, and they would also purify human society. Electricity would restore workers to the countryside. Kipling's "blood-besmeared yellow devils" would yield to liberated workers taking joy in their work. The steam engine tended toward an economy of monopoly and concentration; electricity would promote independence and decentralization.

Mumford wrote *Technics and Civilization* in 1930–31 without ever mentioning the Columbia, but he reintroduced the liberating potential of hydroelectricity, its freeing of human labor and nature, into discussions of hydroelectricity just as the dams became part of Roosevelt's New Deal. What pushed the dams forward to completion, however, was not their ultimate potential for replacing human labor, but their immediate service as an outlet for human labor. Woods, O'Sullivan, Batcheller, and other northwestern boosters and politicians, both Democrats and Republicans, embraced public works as a remedy for unemployment enthusiastically as long as they featured Bonneville and Grand Coulee. The dams would put people back to work.

The ultimate point of this work was a new society. In describing it, politicians and journalists reverted to frontier metaphors that summoned up nature and conquest, old values and new opportunities: a new world open for the taking and remaking. The outcome would be another phase of Frederick Jackson Turner's frontier thesis in which progress sprang from a regression to nature.

Nature was central to this vision in a classically Emersonian way that today seems unlikely to us. We can see the results: a series of giant slack-water ponds, the river's energy turning turbines: pumps lifting its waters into canals, its bed a highway for barges. Herbert Hoover's "maximum utilization," a phrase with neither grace nor beauty, seems a more fitting description than Mumford's vision of the Neotechnic as a world of "ecological balance."

But if the goal is to understand rather than denounce, it is a mistake to read back the fate of the Columbia as a plan to denature it. Billy Clapp, the Ephrata lawyer whom Rufus Woods credited with the idea of a dam at the Grand Coulee, traced his inspiration to secondhand geology from which he learned that glaciers had once dammed the Grand Coulee. In the 1930s proponents of the dams were more likely to see the dams as mimicking nature rather than conquering it. Even engineers thought that way.

Like Hoover, Carl Magnusson was an engineer. He taught at the University of Washington, and in his account nature was Grand Coulee's architect and contractor. The Grand Coulee Dam was but a shadow of an even greater glacial dam that had blocked the river's course and forced it up into the Grand Coulee. Magnusson was perfectly right. What humans intended to do to the river, nature had once done.

The dam will accomplish intentionally the result achieved capriciously by the rampant natural forces of the Pleistocene period. It will raise a portion of the Columbia back into the Coulee, and again the floor of the ancient gorge will be inundated. After being dry and arid throughout almost all the history of mankind, the Grand Coulee once more will be a waterway.

The project, therefore, depended on deciphering the "but-little-understood schemes of Nature." "Nature made the great canal for the project . . ." Nature created the perfect dam site. Nature left the gravel necessary to build the dam. Willis Batcheller, Woods's old ally, picked up the theme. What nature had so artfully arranged, it would be criminal for humans to neglect to improve and finish. The dam was the final piece necessary to reveal nature's latent harmony. "The flood waters come at the same time as the irrigation demand so that there will be no conflict between power and irrigation requirements." Capitalizing on nature, the dam would simultaneously improve it, raising the minimum flow of the river by 50 percent to 10,000 cubic feet per second. Nature had provided the Grand Coulee with "a thick bed of impervious blue clay underlaid by watertight rock," making the coulee watertight. The desert would become a paradise.

From the imitation of nature would come a future electrical millennium. The dam would be, literally and figuratively, "The Biggest Thing on Earth," as Richard Neuberger, the journalist who later became U.S. senator from Oregon, entitled his article for *Harper's* in 1937. Grand Coulee was awash in statistics long before it held back water. Like Superman, it was always greater than its objects of comparison: larger than the Great Pyramid, higher than Niagara, more concrete than a transcontinental highway.

Only the new world it would help produce dwarfed Grand Coulee. Stuart Chase, writing in *Fortune* in 1933, declared that electric power meant a new kind of civilization.

It will shift population, change the map, react—favorably—on ears, eyes, nose and skin cells, profoundly affect both the numbers and the skills of workers, revise—upward—the quality and variety of commodities, break down the division between country man and city man . . . and it promises a world replete with more freedom and happiness than mankind has ever known.

The new continental economy would be "like one unified machine, one organic whole." In this tendency to mix machine, nature, and society into a single metaphorical whole lay a vision of an Emersonian world.

CHAPTER 3
The Power of the River

I

The story, told simply, is that human labor dammed the Columbia so that the river could do work other than its own, so that human beings could live and work differently. Many people invested admirable hopes in these dams. They fought for public control over the energy the dams produced because public power would mean more democratic control over land and resources, more fruitful lives, more pleasant work, and greater returns on labor. They foresaw more intimate human contacts with the natural world and with each other, greater independence and more cohesive communities, an end to crowding, pollution, and waste. Energy, in the form of electricity, became the great good the river could yield. These were not totally failed hopes. We have managed the river to deliver power that has improved lives; the river has also irrigated land and served as a highway for barges. But judged against the larger hopes, our efforts have been failures, and integral to them was a failed relation with nature.

What has failed is our relationship to the river. It is important that we get our metaphors right. We have neither killed the river nor raped it, although people claim both are true. What has happened is closer to a failed marriage. Nature still exists on the Columbia. It is not dead, only altered by our labor. It is the steam within Emerson's boiler. It lies hidden in aluminum factories and pulp mills, in electric lights and washing machines. The organic and mechanical have been merged, as

Lewis Mumford hoped they would, but the results have not been what he intended.

The river is not gone; it is our hopes for it that have vanished. Where Lewis Mumford once imagined utopian futures, we have the Bonneville Power Administration (BPA), a public agency that exists to transmit electricity to markets and to create markets to which it can transmit electricity. The progressive hopes it once embodied have given way to excuses; new possibilities have become hard choices. Utopianism has yielded to a self-serving bureaucratic and corporate fatalism. We have not killed the river; we have disappointed ourselves.

Nor have we raped the river. As a metaphor, rape replicates the very cultural categories of feminine nature/masculine culture that block understanding. It plays only on surface similarities. Construction is often violent and intrusive. To create the Grand Coulee Dam and the Bonneville Dam the federal government, through the Bureau of Reclamation and the Army Corps of Engineers, employed consortiums of construction companies to organize the regimented labor of men and their machines. These men and machines physically cut and entered the river. They bared its bed.

Through labor the river was tactilely known, visually known, and this now purely visual, artfully constructed knowledge is still available to us. Photographers represented and commemorated work in tens of thousands of pictures of the great dams. Each photograph is an artifact of the space between the camera and its object. Those taken from a distance emphasize the abstract: geometric shapes of scaffolding, the linear surface of the cofferdam, the bulk of the great dam itself rising in the river, the more irregular shape of the Columbia's cliffs and bluffs. Photographs of the middle distance reveal machines and actual construction. The machines lift and push and trundle earth and rock from one place and deposit it in another. The landscape seems one vast ruin. Only in the close-ups do humans appear, and then they are everywhere. In these pictures men strain, lift, and carry; they dangle from cliffs and from the dam itself; they perch on steel beams and climb scaffolds.

In many of these pictures the connection between labor and nature appears as intimate and dangerous as anything experienced more than a century earlier. When workers suspended themselves from cliffs, their lives depended on knowledge of the rock. When workers dangled from the dam, the river surged beneath them. When workers stripped the last of the rotten bedrock from the riverbed by hand, they had to know where to pry, learn what was solid and what would crack. When workers took cores from the bedrock, they bared the river's foundations and its past.

In damming the river, the workers knew nature through labor. It is foolish to deny that the men who bored the bedrock, who walked the river bottom, who came to know with fine precision the density and composition of the clay, sand, and granite of the river were in a full and meaningful sense knowing nature. It is foolish to think that the danger and exhilaration of a man dangling from a cliff with a jackhammer somehow differs from that of rock climbers who also dangle from cliffs. We need to take the work and its intent seriously.

The workers left few published accounts about this knowledge: what they intended, thought, or felt. They do not say whether they came to love the rock they transformed; whether through their labor the river entered their bone, sinew, and brain until later those moments dangling between rock and water would seem the most real and vital of their lives. The children of some of these workers know their stories of these days. They know their pride was this dam. For others it was just a job, a wage, a biding of time, neither love nor rape.

A century earlier Astorians told their own stories of the river; journalists and writers of government publications told the workers' stories. And writers commemorating the dam leaped almost instinctively to connect the twentieth-century workers with the first Europeans to reach the region. In such accounts workers were "frontiersmen" subduing a feminine nature. Such analogies are, of course, flawed even beyond their gendering. The Columbia Basin had already been fully settled by Indians: it had been nearly fully settled and largely abandoned by farmers, the ruins of whose efforts were everywhere. Nevertheless, to publicists and journalists the Columbia Basin became the last American frontier. The second wave of farmers moving onto reclaimed land were still pioneers. This "last frontier where men vie with the forces of nature," as a 1947 promotional brochure put it, was "a man's world."

Here again were the elements of metaphorical rape: men vying with female nature, a relationship ultimately determined by force. But the actual working out of the frontier metaphors often took place in conscious opposition to the older visions of the conquest of nature. The journalist Katherine Glover placed the dams at the end of the Oregon

Trail on a "social and a physical frontier." But success would not be measured by a duplication of old patterns. Instead, settlers would acknowledge the mistakes in older relationships with nature, "evolving and using new ways of work and life."

Here, as with the rhetoric advocating dams, the emphasis was on mimicking and not conquering nature. The logic was Emersonian. The dams represented a marriage of nature and machine; they represented new beginnings for modern Dust Bowl refugees and eastern slum dwellers. People in the new Northwest were, Glover wrote, "returning to begin again like the salmon."

This connection between human work and the work of salmon struggling upstream was not just an idiosyncratic conceit of Glover's. In "Talking Columbia," Woody Guthrie pondered the Columbia, "a river just goin' to waste" while "folks need houses and stuff to eat, and the folks need the metals and the folks need wheat. Folks need water and power dams. Folks need people and the people need the land. The whole big Pacific Northwest up in here ought to be run, way I see it, by e-lec-tri-city . . ."

Politicians in the East, Guthrie sang, derided this dream of "electricity runnin' all around, cheaper than rainwater," but "them boys didn't know their royal chinooks." Guthrie "figured all those salmon just couldn't be wrong." A good river for salmon was a good river for power and would be a good river for working Americans. Here, too, salmon served as a metaphor for the promise of the dams. More than half a century later comparing humans and salmon seems an oddly obtuse metaphor. But in building the dams that would ravage the salmon runs, humans compared themselves to salmon. They were working the river, coming back to a land renewed by electricity.

Woody Guthrie himself came to the Columbia in 1941 with the forlorn hope that the Bonneville Power Administration might give him a starring role in a documentary about the Columbia. What he got was a month's work at a common laborer's wage. Woody Guthrie was not a worker, but he wrote eloquently of work. And, perhaps, salmon advocating dams is no more unlikely a possibility than Woody Guthrie driving around in a BPA car writing songs about the Columbia. Guthrie wrote more than twenty songs: stirring, rousing, evocative songs. A man who hardly knew the Columbia created the century's most lasting images of the river. He wrote songs of work and energy and of a new world being born. They are not songs of raping a river.

Guthrie exalted work. He wrote back to Pete Seeger and others in New York City that if songs were to reach workers, they needed to put "wheels, whistles, steam, boilers, shafts, cranks, operators, tuggers, pulleys [and] engines" in them. Guthrie vividly rendered work, yet the workers themselves, as in other contemporary accounts of the dams, were anonymous.

Rape depersonalizes its victim, but it is the workers who become oddly depersonalized in even sympathetic accounts of the dams. There were about seven thousand of them employed at the Grand Coulee at the peak of construction. Although closer to us in time and experience than the Astorians, they seem more distant, less individualized, more shadowy than Astor's men with their vivid, personal stories. Workers appear en masse: workers lining up for their pay, for their meals. They are reduced to part of the barrage of statistics that surrounded the dam. We know they were young men. In 1937 nearly 60 percent of them were under thirty; the majority of them were unmarried. The sum of their experience was the 100 million man-hours of work that went into the dam. Only occasionally names appear to go with the thousands of pictures: Harvey Henke, Louie Eylar, Clayton Hanson. But there is no other information. They exist in the pamphlets, the brochures, the publicity shots as representative types. Only their work seems to matter. Their work was their identity: it could be classified, subdivided, and marked. Colors identified workers by job. There were sixteen different classifications. Cooling-pipe men wore green hats; carpenters, laborers, and concrete men wore red; electricians wore a combination of red, green, and blue.

Their deaths on the job became as depersonalized as their lives. Seventy-seven of them died, mostly from falling or from having something fall on them. The deaths were just more grist for the Grand Coulee's statistical mill: 22 million yards of earth excavated, 127 miles of steel piling in the west cofferdam alone, 10.5 million board feet of heavy timbers for the cofferdam cribs, and 77 dead. In building the dam they were the epitome of the mass society that Mumford hoped to displace.

II

In a sense the Columbia River dams made the Pacific Northwest a region. The lines of the Bonneville Power Administration marked the region's boundaries. Where interties with other transmission systems occurred, there the Pacific Northwest encountered other regions. Electricity represented an extension of the river's reach. The Columbia would help illuminate places that contributed no water to its flow. But, in turn, lights going on in those places shaped what happened on the river. These things did not simply happen; they were planned.

Planning was critical to the river, but plans for the Columbia rarely regarded it as anything more than an abstraction, a prime mover providing potential kilowatts. Planners reduced the essential river to a statistic—42 percent of the country's total hydropower capacity. Only at rare moments did the actual river break through. Those moments— when its beauty astonished, when its power destroyed, when the life it supported changed—challenged the planners, who, nonetheless, never lost faith in a fully rationalized river, an organic machine.

Lewis Mumford was not a planner, but he wrote eloquently of planning. It was a difficult task. Planning is an exercise of power, and in a modern state much real power is suffused with boredom. The agents of planning are usually boring; the planning process is boring; the implementation of plans is always boring. In a democracy boredom works for bureaucracies and corporations as smell works for a skunk. It keeps danger away. Power does not have to be exercised behind the scenes. It can be open. The audience is asleep. The modern world is forged amidst our inattention.

In the 1930s Mumford wrote *The Culture of Cities* and called for "the re-animation and re-building of regions as deliberate works of collective art." This was the "grand task of politics for the opening generation." The world was stirring and the opportunity to remodel the earth and society was at hand. Already in the power dams and great highways one could feel "the thrust and sweep of the new creative imagination." Mumford was revolted at the "shapeless giantism" of a metropolitan life that lacked the cultural and the natural resources to sustain itself. He saw the new technics as a way to escape the "Plutonian world" of industrialism and achieve a "life centered order" which would focus on the reproduction of living communities instead of the cancerous growth of the metropolis.

Lewis Mumford had never visited the Pacific Northwest when Benjamin Kizer, the chair of the Washington State Planning Council, wrote him that *The Culture of Cities* was "causing young men to see visions and old men to dream dreams." Kizer asked him to advise the Pacific Northwest Regional Planning Commission (PNWRPC). Mumford came in 1938.

The PNWRPC was a way station on a real, if circuitous, path to social power. The commission created many of the blueprints for future regional development. Its planning activities were not just airy dreams and empty discussions. The PNWRPC had for several years been arguing that the Columbia was a "regional stream" that must be at the heart of any regional planning effort. Mumford wrote a memorandum for the PNWRPC valuable less for its actual influence (although Kizer at least took Mumfordian positions) than for its astute assessment of the forces in play on the river in 1938.

The Bonneville Project Act passed by Congress in 1937 was, in part, the work of the PNWRPC. It had recommended the formation of a federal corporation entrusted with "the operation of the federal power facilities, including the development of the power market and the sale of power at wholesale." Despite all the efforts to create a Columbia Valley Authority modeled after the TVA, the PNWRPC recognized that the West was not the South. The Tennessee Valley had no equivalents to the Bureau of Reclamation and the Army Corps of Engineers, large bureaucratic players on the river who could not be easily displaced. There was, however, an empty niche—the long-distance transmission of electricity. The Bonneville Power Act created a federal agency, the Bonneville Power Project (which became the Bonneville Power Administration in 1940), to transmit and wholesale electricity through a system that would eventually link the Bonneville and the Grand Coulee and subsequent dams on the river and its tributaries.

The dams and the Bonneville Project had made the river an ideological battleground. Planners saw the Columbia as the key to "the entire program of water and land use and general progress," but it was the nature of the program that was at issue. The goal of progressives was to make "socially desirable uses economically practicable." They regarded public power as a weapon against monopoly and political corruption. They wanted coordinated development with decentralization of population and industry. They wanted public transmission and so-called postage-stamp rates (a low uniform wholesale rate across the entire area), for such rates would secure wide use. And, finally, they desired the retailing of power through nonprofit public agencies. They were particularly enamored with Public Utility Districts (PUDs), nonprofit elected bodies that would market power at cost.

Mumford was a progressive, but he feared mere rate making would replace real planning. The construction of the electrical grid, whose main transmission lines would initially form a great triangle linking Spokane, Seattle, and Portland, would create new possibilities but not necessarily optimum outcomes. He called advocates of uniform rates the "spread it everywhere" school. They treated electricity like fertilizer. But it was the planner and not the market alone that should decide where industry and population grew.

Private utilities, allied with the Portland Chamber of Commerce and the Army Corps of Engineers, formed a powerful opposing coalition. They were conservatives who thought in terms of existing structures; they desired piecemeal development which focused on the most lucrative opportunities and preserved the social status quo. Mumford ridiculed them as guardians of the Paleotechnic. The "industrial development at any price" school, which treated electrical power as if it suffered from the "same disabilities as steam and coal" and was best used near its site of production, had allied itself with the "continued congestion for profit" school. They sought to concentrate population in existing cities, where it was already congested and poorly housed.

The progressives and conservatives clashed in local elections, in Congress, and at bureaucratic hearings. Normally arcane or technical issues such as rate making or electrical transmission took on heavy ideological weight and became centers of public debate. The progressives won on virtually every key issue. They forged a system based on wide use, federal transmission of power, public preference, and virtual postage-stamp rates. They envisioned the disappearance of private utilities.

The appointment of James D. Ross as the first head of the Bonneville Project seemed to secure the triumph of public power. In an age before the term became an oxymoron, Ross, former head of Seattle City Light, was a charismatic bureaucrat. When a Seattle mayor fired him, the voters recalled the mayor. Ross was reinstated. Franklin Roosevelt admired him inordinately; in appointing him to lead the Bonneville Project, he picked a man who wanted low federal power rates to be a yardstick for all utility rates. Ross barnstormed the Northwest holding hearings and garnering popular support for virtual postage-stamp rates for Bonneville.

The Bonneville Act itself contained a clause directing the Bonneville Project to give preference to publicly owned systems in all sales. The existing public systems were far too small to absorb this electricity, but the preference clause gave new life to an older campaign for public power. Reformers put particularly great hope in organizing new PUDs. Washington voters approved numerous PUDs; Oregon voters, operating under more restrictive legislation and influenced by a powerful conservative opposition that argued the PUDs would increase local taxes, created relatively few.

PUDs and postage-stamp rates are now exactly the kind of issues that make the eyes glaze and the mind wander. They are technical and abstract, but once they provoked passion. Indeed, in the planning documents of the 1930s, they often seem more real than the physical river, which almost disappeared among the kilowatts and acre-feet of water which are nature's energy and nature itself abstracted and commodified. The planners allocated these commodities and calculated the results.

Only at its most spectacular did the river succeed in forcing itself through the calculations to demand attention. The place that gripped even the planners was the Columbia Gorge, the site of the Bonneville Dam, where the river cut the Cascades. Mumford was fascinated by the gorge. It crystallized his own Emersonian ideas about nature; in his memorandum the preservation of the gorge became a crucial test of regional planning. The gorge, where Kipling had seen Chinese at work, unrolled itself to Mumford "like some great kakemono of classic Chinese landscape art." Kipling had made the gorge the site of an elemental clash between nature and work, but Mumford posed a more complicated relation between the natural and the social. He thought that "nature is no longer an absolute: or rather, we no longer regard nature as if man himself were not implicated in her, as if his modifications of nature were not themselves a part of the natural order to which he is born." This Emersonian premise allowed Mumford to celebrate dams and hydroelectricity even as he put limits on them. Development threatened, Mumford wrote, to "deface the natural beauty of this extraordinary site beyond repair." Machines in Mumford's Paleotechnic had simplified the organic, but the time had come for the organic to "complicate the mechanical . . . to make it more organic [and] . . . more harmonious with our living environment." Planners must (and did) stave off the Paleotechnic hands reaching for the Neotechnic levers.

Nature was central but not sacred for Mumford, Ross, and progressive planners; nature demanded loving transformation. Regional planning sought "to bring the earth as a whole up to the highest pitch of perfection and appropriate use." For Mumford such use had to have room for Thoreau's sauntering: the "glimpse of sun, . . . taste of wind, . . . smell of earth, . . . growing things, . . . free play of muscles and . . . spontaneous pleasure." Planners and thinkers needed to orient themselves around the "realities of organic life." In an advanced society nature became an active component of culture, and culture, in turn, "became a second nature."

Mumford judged the Columbia Gorge perfect and appropriate as it was, but most of the earth needed tinkering. Science provided the tools, such as electricity; "rational human values" provided the ends for regional planning's higher exploitation of the earth.

But here was the rub. What were the rational human values that would guide the endeavor? Mumford was hardly a technological determinist. The building of a dam did not produce a better world. The machine made new modes of life possible, but unless humans were already "better than the machine," they would be reduced to its level: "dumb, servile, abject, a creature of immediate reflexes and passive unselective responses."

At the end of Mumford's century, his fumbling for a source of popular values to guide planning seems naive and circular. Education would create people with "humanist attitudes, cooperative methods, rational controls" all linked by a common feeling for the landscape and a common regional culture. Without such people who knew "where they live and how they live" planning would be "a barren externalism." This was edifying: it was also contradictory and obscurantist. If regional planners depended on such a cultural base to plan, and if that cultural base had to be created through a sort of Deweyian education, then regional planning would seemingly have to go into a generational hold. But regional planning was going on, and Mumford vigorously advocated it. And since the regionally sensitive population remained to be created, planning couldn't be, in Mumfordian terms, democratic; it could only be what it often seemed, mandarin. When local people agreed with planners, they were evidence of a vigorous regional culture. When they disagreed, they were representatives of narrow local interest.

Mumfordian planning stumbled on its own contradictions, but planning, nonetheless, triumphed. What has happened on the Columbia over the last half century has been planned. It has not yielded a vibrant regional culture. Planning has not been democratic. It has not linked people with the land. It has, however, been spectacularly successful in changing the relations of the region to the nation as a whole.

As the chairman of the National Resources Board told the mayor of Portland in 1933: "Planning does not, in this instance, or in general, involve changes in the existing economic system or social order." Planners, politicians, and businesspeople agreed that the Columbia should become the engine that powered factories, lighted cities, and irrigated the land. It would help free the region from its colonial dependence on the East, liberating it from its role as a provider of raw materials. BPA planners in the Division of Industrial and Resources Development and cooperating agencies surveyed resources and possible plant sites, assessed labor conditions and the likelihood of strikes, targeted possible industries, and allocated power resources.

Growth, particularly industrial growth, was the goal. Ross and other progressives were more committed to growth, more confident it could be attained, than the conservatives. Ross was certain that markets existed for all the electricity the Columbia could produce. The agency's job was to deliver it. As he told an audience at St. Helens, Oregon:

. . . the function of Bonneville is to bring to you a great supply of current so that you can be assured of getting it and when it runs out, by that time Coulee will be done and the two interconnected can bring you some more power, and when they are done there is the Snake River in Idaho, and the more dams on the Columbia and the more dams that go up on the Snake the more help it will give you people.

The Northwest would need power for mining, to process raw materials to "make a lot of things of metal that are made in the East." Power

would provide irrigation and make phosphate fertilizers to restore fertility
to exhausted land. Electricity would alleviate what Senator George
Norris of Nebraska called "the unending punishing tasks" of rural life.
Electricity would finally reduce the drudgery and hard labor of farm
women who carried endless buckets of water drawn from hand pumps.
Electric washers and irons would replace zinc washboards and flatirons
heated on stoves. Electric lights would brighten farmhouses; radios
would enliven them. Electricity would spread out into the dairy and
other areas of the farm, reducing male as well as female labor. Paul
Raver, Ross's successor, took even more pains to stimulate and encourage demand. He shared the conviction of the necessity for constantly increasing production.

In the 1930s the Northwest was still a poor, hardscrabble place, full
of resentments against the East. The lust for growth the dams unleashed
seemed almost elemental, and to control it progressives needed a social
vision of the same raw strength. What some of them embraced instead
was a pious, essentially backward-looking rural nostalgia. Roosevelt told
Harold Ickes, his Secretary of the Interior, that future farmers in the
Columbia Basin should be "raising what they can of their own food,
canning the surplus for their own use, perhaps even making their own
shoes and certain types of clothing." Morris L. Cooke, so influential
in shaping Gifford Pinchot's Giant Power program in Pennsylvania,
became the first head of the Rural Electrification Administration. He
thought that the dominance of " 'city people' in human affairs and the
lessening influence of those in material and spiritual touch with the
soil" lay at the root of modern problems.

World War II delayed construction on the Columbia Basin Project;
inflation and drainage problems increased its cost, and to this day, huge
as it is, the project remains only partially complete. It did not produce
the "modern rural community of a million people, possibly many
more," in the Columbia Basin that boosters predicted. And in the end,
the project had little in common with the fantasies of Roosevelt or
Cooke and much to do with the realities of capitalist agriculture. From
the beginning the settlers on the project were neither young nor poor.
In the mid-1950s a third did not even live on their farms, and only 40
percent of the farms were operated by their owners. The farms were,
nonetheless, heavily subsidized—power users and the government paid
84 percent of the irrigation costs. With dropping commodity prices and

rising costs, these subsidized farmers demanded an end to acreage limitations originally imposed on the project to minimize speculation and
maximize resettlement. In 1957 Congress raised the limit to 160 acres
and 320 acres for a married couple. Farmers could lease additional
land. In 1982 the limit rose to 960 acres and Congress dropped the
requirement that those receiving water had to live within fifty miles of
the project. The government abandoned any pretense of decentralization, small family farms, or rural reform.

The Columbia Basin Project did not so much eliminate the punishing
tasks of rural life as redistribute them. By 1952, 97 percent of the farms
in the BPA service area had electricity. Electricity reduced the labor of
farm owners and their families, but on the irrigated landscape it created,
migrant workers took over hard and often dangerous work. Dams had
created the opportunity for new, electrified family farms, but Mexican
and Mexican-American seasonal workers labored in their fields for
wages. They often lived in farm labor camps that made unelectrified
farmhouses seem bastions of comfort.

With decentralization reduced to a rural nostalgia seemingly incapable of preventing the replication of the very injustices it hoped to
remedy, growth easily took leave of social reform. Paul Raver still talked
in 1944 of "social and cultural betterment and improvement of gov-
ernmental and cooperative machinery," but ultimately such sentiments
were merely decorative. The technical heart of the vision of controlling
the river kept beating in BPA studies or in the massive report on the
future of the Columbia issued by the Bureau of Reclamation in 1947.
The reformist soul had fled. The social ends electricity was meant to
achieve, so clear in the 1930s, largely vanished from the discussion of
development. Electricity had become an end in itself. As *The Northwest
Ruralite*, a newsletter for members of rural electric cooperatives, put
it: "electric power is like love—nobody ever gets quite enough."

After the war the BPA became an agency devoted to supplying power
at the lowest possible cost, planning its distribution, and stimulating
the market. Above all, the agency worked to secure its own growth. It
became, in short, a successful public authority similar to numerous
other public authorities across the United States.

The mature BPA has never had a single dominating figure who shaped
the region the way Robert Moses shaped New York. James D. Ross
died too soon after taking office, and subsequent leaders have been

bland and rather faceless. Important and clever men such as Bernard Goldhammer, eventually Bonneville's power manager, were not widely known outside the agency. The BPA is a large and boring agency, and boredom has served it well. There are few serious studies of the agency; its histories are its own. But there is no ignoring the BPA. It has made the modern Columbia. It has been relentlessly obedient to one part of its original charter: "encourage the widest possible use of all electric energy that can be generated and marketed." Hydropower was good, clean, and renewable. There could never be too much of such a good thing.

This growth certainly served national and regional interests; it created new opportunities for human labor. During World War II, electricity from the dams went almost totally to defense. National defense, in turn, gave the region the industrial base it so longed for. The dams powered the shipyards of Portland, Vancouver, and Seattle, the aluminum mills the Defense Plant Corporation built across the Northwest, and the factories that turned aluminum into airplanes. They supplied power to the top secret project at Hanford which was producing plutonium for the atomic bomb dropped on Nagasaki. It was federal investment and federal power that freed the Pacific Northwest from being a hewer of wood and drawer of water for the East.

The growth of the BPA and the economic growth of the region did not, however, mean that public power triumphed as a friend of democracy and an enemy of monopoly. The great opportunity for public power to drive private utilities from the field came before the war, and it was not ready. The public market had not yet materialized when the Bonneville (1938) and the Grand Coulee (1941) came on line. Then the war came and put the agency's public preference clause on hold. Less than 10 percent of the BPA's revenues between 1940 and 1945 came from public-power customers. It would not be until 1952 that the BPA sold more electricity to public customers than to investor-owned utilities (IOUs), and even then the combination of direct industrial and private utility sales continued to dwarf public preference sales.

Aluminum—the Neotechnic metal Mumford so much admired—took the power from the dams and sent Mumford's organic machine spinning wildly out of control. Aluminum plants owned by a few large corporations made a mockery of the project's mandate to provide the widest possible use and avoid the monopolization of electricity. But the war forced new priorities. Aluminum was vital to the aircraft industry. And so aluminum came in 1943 to consume 60 percent of the megawatt-hours the BPA sold. The BPA and Secretary Ickes did not concede everything. They defeated a plan for a single huge Alcoa plant in Spokane. Instead the Defense Plant Corporation built several plants and sold them to different operators after the war at fire-sale prices.

Aluminum had, however, hijacked the river. As the war ended and defense demands for aluminum declined, the BPA's own industrial sales policy promoted production. Economically and politically, the BPA depended on its power sales to aluminum producers. Through the 1940s aluminum would continue to absorb roughly half the electricity transmitted by the BPA. Aluminum also contributed mightily to the power shortages that threatened the region in 1948 and again in 1952 and repeatedly thereafter. In 1970 the aluminum industry consumed 22 billion kilowatt-hours, 40 percent of the energy sold by the BPA. Eventually aluminum alone would consume an energy output equivalent to five Bonneville Dams. Despite the BPA commitment to the "expansion and stabilization of local employment," these plants brought relatively few jobs. Whether huge blocks of power should be diverted to a single industry was not really a question asked much following the war. Aluminum was necessary for national defense, and into the 1980s Bonneville provided power for one-third of American smelting capacity.

The BPA's relationship with private utilities was far rockier than its relationship with industrial purchasers. World War II had forced a shotgun wedding that united the public and private power sources into a single integrated supply system that ran over BPA lines: the Northwest Power Pool. A strong public-power culture remained within the agency, but a preference for public development yielded to the political necessity of compromise with the IOUs in order to meet the everyday demands of managing the river.

The BPA and the IOUs had a common cause in stimulating and rationalizing demand. Like any successful utility system, the BPA sought to avoid high peaks and deep valleys of power use. Because electricity cannot be stored, productive capacity necessary for the peaks had to stand expensively idle when demand sank into the valleys. In a hydropower system, this meant that water flowed uselessly over the top of the dams. The idea was to think of new forms of consumption to fill, at least partially, the valleys. All-electric houses, new appliances, better street lighting, electric trains, all helped to diversify demand and spread the electrical load. Between 1938 and 1952 energy use for residential purposes quadrupled while the actual cost of electricity was cut in half.

Increased demand for electricity, of course, also contributed to power shortages, but this served to point out the still huge untapped potential of the Columbia: "Energy Equal to 15,000 Oil Wells Flows Wasted into the Sea." The BPA, the Army Corps of Engineers, and the Bureau of Reclamation all wanted more dams. But amidst postwar retrenchment and conservative hostility to public power, even previously approved dams had to fight hard for funding. Then the river itself came to the aid of dam builders.

The Columbia, so often an abstraction of kilowatts and firm and interruptible power, did an uncharacteristic thing in 1948: it flooded. The Columbia is not the Missouri or the Mississippi. It does not have a long history of flooding. The Columbia rose every spring and early summer, and its freshets inundated low-lying bottomland, but there had been great floods only in 1876 and 1894. By 1948 few remembered them. And as the region developed, particularly as it developed during the war, people built and farmed on lands safe from all but the great floods.

The river crested in June 1948 well below the record flood of 1894 in which Captain Martineau had tried to run his steamboat up the Cascades, but it did far more damage. It killed thirty-eight people and destroyed $103 million worth of property. Where once there had been forest, marsh, and swamp, there were now farms, factories, highways, and cities. There was, above all, Vanport.

It didn't take long to create Vanport—then, with 20,000 people, the second-largest city in Oregon. Henry Kaiser, the industrialist who grew wealthy from government contracts, had built the community for the government. It housed the workers he brought in for the shipyards at Vancouver and Portland during the war. Sitting on the floodplain at the mouth of the Willamette across the Columbia from Vancouver, Washington, Vanport depended on dikes as jerry-built as the town itself. When a railway embankment, part of the dike system, collapsed, the river surged through, and when it receded, Vanport went with it. Miraculously only a few lives were lost, but in a single hour on a sunny May afternoon, the Columbia had destroyed the second-largest city in

Oregon. To Woody Guthrie, then vacationing at the Stonecrest Lodge—"a radical Working Class Island up here in a Lake of Dead Moneybellies"—the river no longer seemed benevolent. But his program for the river was the same. The lack of flood control and power dams "will give us all plenty to make up songs and to sing about for the rest of our native lives."

The flood both helped and frustrated the BPA. It helped halt cutbacks in the BPA budget and staff. It speeded funding for the completion of the McNary and Hungry Horse dams and prompted the authorization of new dams. But the effect was temporary. In the 1950s the Eisenhower administration adopted a policy of "no new starts" for federal projects while providing tax incentives for private development. But even under this policy Congress funded the dams authorized under Truman.

Despite the obstacles placed in its path, the agency grew more powerful. With political help from Washington's senators, Henry Jackson and Warren Magnuson, the BPA survived and adapted. The BPA retained its preeminent role as the planner and promoter of regional growth. It was the responsibility of the BPA to plan for more power well in advance of the region's needs. The agency itself could not build dams, and attempts to form a successor agency that could failed. But the BPA retained its critical control over transmission and coordination. It gave up ambitions to eliminate private utilities and instead accommodated them. Beginning with the Priest Rapids Dam in 1957, joint ventures between public agencies and private utilities created new dams on the middle Columbia, but under a "wheeling" agreement passed by Congress, the BPA transmitted their power. These dams made some PUDs major power producers, but smaller PUDs became little more than administrative appendages of the BPA. Once celebrated as agencies of democratic control, the PUDs eventually were ridiculed as a refuge for rubes where experts played on the ambitions and gullibility of small-town businesspeople.

Dams came on line at the rate of one to three a year between 1952 and 1958. And as the partnership policy of the Eisenhower administration weakened, new authorizations brought a second burst of federal dam building starting in the late 1950s. Eventually the federal government and public utilities (which developed the main stem) and the private utilities (which concentrated on the tributaries) plugged most major dam sites on the Columbia and its tributaries with earth or concrete. Only the Hanford Reach remained undammed. All this power flowed into a network managed by the BPA.

The BPA blueprint for development grew ever more ambitious. The distinctions between predicting growth and promoting it, between planning and boosting have always been fine ones in the West. The BPA's short-term estimates of power needs proved reasonably accurate, and this gave credence to their dreamier long-term predictions. In 1954, Gus Norwood, later a historian of the BPA, cited "conservative" predictions by General Electric that by the year 2000 the BPA would require some forty-five Grand Coulee Dams to serve the Pacific Northwest alone. The rising demand would require an equivalent of the Dalles Dam, then under construction, every year of the 1960s. And then, when all the hydro sources were harnessed, the BPA would rely on atomic power. With demand so huge and certain, public responsibility dictated building ahead of the demand, with a 10 percent reserve always on hand.

By the 1970s the agency had taken giant steps toward rationalizing the river. It had created a huge organic machine to produce power. In 1970 it distributed the electricity from twenty-six federal dams on the Columbia or its tributaries, with five more under construction and two others authorized. It had received over $4.6 billion in congressional appropriations and paid back nearly $1.7 billion. It united public utilities, private utilities, and direct industrial consumers in a single Columbia River power system.

Planning had become a blueprint for growth; the river had become the machinery of growth, but the process was not yet complete. Postwar planners dropped the rhetoric of conforming to nature's design. The Columbia, whose rise to its peak in late spring and summer seemed to early promoters so in tune with the needs of agriculture, was indifferent to demands for power. Seventy-three percent of the normal flow of the river came during the six summer months, only 27 percent in the winter, when regional demands for power were highest. At full flow, the water was wasted. At low water, there was not enough flow to meet demand. The goal was to even out the flow, to make it conform to human needs rather than the rhythms of rain and melting snow. For this, storage was necessary.

The initial postwar development of the Columbia had emphasized run-of-the-river power sites over storage sites. Like Bonneville, these

run-of-the-river dams produced electricity according to the natural fluctuations of the river. Further rationalization of the river involved increasing firm power by holding water in storage like so much liquid
fuel and releasing it at times of peak power demand. Storage would
increase the "firm output" always available at the dams as distinguished
from the "secondary output," which was available only at times of peak
flow. The river would flow when and where managers desired it to
flow.

The Grand Coulee provided the model for how the whole river system
would ideally work. By releasing stored water during winter periods of
normally low flow, the Grand Coulee doubled the firm power that
could be generated at six power sites between the dam and the Snake
as well as boosting by 50 percent the firm power of Bonneville. But the
Grand Coulee, enormous as it was, did not have sufficient storage
capacity to rationalize the river adequately. And part of its water, in
any case, had to be pumped out of the river as irrigation projects came
on line.

Storage seemed the solution to increasing power, but unfortunately
there were no more storage sites available on the river's main stem
within the United States. There was storage capacity on the tributaries,
but new projects there threatened fisheries, wildlife, and national parks.
And in any case, the Eisenhower administration was unwilling to fund
new federal storage projects and the PUDs and IOUs had no economic
incentive to do so.

To further rationalize the river, planners would have to circumvent
national boundaries. Power plants were in the United States; storage
sites were in Canada. Planning became diplomacy in the Columbia
River Treaty of 1964. Three new Canadian dams, which could also
eventually produce power, would hold back the Columbia's flow, di-
minishing flood danger and releasing the water downstream as required
by power dams in the United States. The amount of firm power at
existing dams would increase by approximately 2.8 million kilowatts,
the rough equivalent of another Grand Coulee Dam. The Canadians
received half the new power the American dams produced as well as
payment for flood-control benefits. They, in turn, agreed to sell this
British Columbia Power Entitlement in the United States on contracts
running for thirty years. The American down payment on this power
was enough to build the dams.

To work, the treaty depended on the coordination of all producers on the river and a complicated exchange brokered by the BPA. In what would become a common BPA technique, the BPA acquired all of the British Columbia Power Entitlement, thus absorbing the risk, while promising purchasers firm power from its own supply. The BPA then marketed surpluses the treaty produced to California through a new intertie.

The Columbia Treaty gave the BPA a new source of power, and this power became revenue through the $700 million intertie with California authorized in 1964. Pacific Northwesterners feared California's ambitions to divert part of the river south, but they wanted, at least temporarily, California markets for Columbia power. The California market could absorb not only the new Canadian power but also an estimated $30 million worth of secondary power then unmarketable in the Northwest. Protective legislation maintained the Northwest's preferential access to federal hydropower.

The BPA badly needed this revenue. It was long the boast and a significant political strength of the agency that every cent invested in it by the federal government was returned with interest. By 1956, however, the high cost of new dams and changes in accounting procedures had begun to cut into net revenues. In 1958 the drain of depreciation and interest expenses produced the first deficit in the agency's history. Deficits became chronic into the mid-1960s, although the agency's cumulative revenues still exceeded expenses.

Together the Columbia River Treaty and the intertie promised to correct a system in danger of double deficits of power and revenue. The intertie created a more heterogeneous and varied set of power demands. When supply exceeded demand in one area, it could be transmitted to another where demand exceeded supply. And when conditions were reversed, the flow of electricity could be reversed. A utility did not need to produce enough power to meet peak demands if it could depend on the BPA to divert excess power to it. The intertie with California allowed the flow of the Columbia to power air conditioners to cool the California summer while using California energy in low-water years to guarantee the power that brightened the long winter nights of the Pacific Northwest; up and down the coast natural and social systems were all to be calibrated, matched, and made part of the grid. Snow melting, dams storing and releasing water, turbines turning, generators producing elec-

tricity, lights going on, motors humming all blended together; the Columbia seemed a single well-managed machine. Its reach extended from
the Canadian Rockies to southern California. It was an incredible technical achievement; it worked day after day, month after month, year
after year.

But no matter how rationalized the river became, how closely linked
with human labor and its products, it remained a natural system with
a logic of its own. When, as in 1972–73, winter storms did not produce
sufficient snowpack and drought followed in spring and summer, reservoirs declined, and energy production fell. Reservoirs could not store
water that nature did not produce, and as of September 1, 1973, the
reservoirs were 15 million kilowatt-hours below normal operating level.
There was an even worse drought in 1976.

Low water meant less energy to sell and the necessity of buying energy
outside the system. By 1973, the agency was running record deficits.
Even a rationalized river was in the end a creature of nature's flux.
With a nearly fully dammed Columbia incapable of meeting future
demands for energy, the BPA looked for new sources of power that
could compensate for the river's fluctuations. They planned to build
thermal plants to run in tandem with hydro plants. Once on line,
thermal plants would supply the base load with hydro plants coming
in to supply peak demands.

Thermal plants in the BPA's planning came increasingly to mean
nuclear plants, and nuclear plants became synonymous with the Washington Public Power Supply System (WPPSS—pronounced "Whoops"
in Washington). In 1962, Senator Henry Jackson had bought off private-
power opposition to production of electricity by a new dual-purpose
reactor at the federal reservation at Hanford by promising half the power,
risk-free, to private utilities. WPPSS, a consortium of public utilities,
built the generating facilities that turned steam from the reactor into
electricity. The BPA secured the arrangement by promising firm power
to WPPSS in exchange for whatever power the dual reactor could
produce. Although the capacity of the reactor was equal to two Bonneville Dams, the reactor itself proved unreliable and its power expensive.

Problems with the dual-purpose reactor did not faze either the BPA
or WPPSS. In 1969 the Joint Power Planning Council, chaired by BPA
administrator H. R. Richmond and largely run by BPA staff, set up a
ten-year $7 billion program involving regional utilities and the BPA.

Central to the plan were three nuclear reactors to be built by WPPSS. The BPA, as usual, brokered the deal, created a complicated accounting system—net billing—that avoided the legal prohibition against Bonneville purchases of nonfederal power, and subsidized high-priced nuclear power while providing funds to WPPSS. Through net billing Bonneville absorbed most of the risk that the first three reactors might never produce electricity. Then in 1976 it presented customers with forecasts of future power shortages so dire that the PUDs agreed to build two more nuclear reactors. But because of an IRS decision and the financial condition of the BPA, net billing was impossible for the final two plants. WPPSS assumed full risk.

The result was an enormous fiasco. "No one," a Bonneville official admitted, "anticipated how hard it would be to build these turkeys." Inflation hurt, but the plants were also poorly designed and cavalierly supervised. By 1979, WPPSS was $7.75 billion over budget and rising. By 1981, original estimates on the costs of the five plants had soared from $5 billion to $24 billion. In nominal dollars, at least, the reactors eventually cost more than the entire Columbia River Power System: its dams, transmission lines, and substations. Abandoning construction of the final two plants produced the greatest bond default in American history. Only one of the first three reactors has ever produced electricity. Absorbing its share of the costs of WPPSS contributed heavily to a sixfold increase in BPA rates between 1979 and 1983.

The demand the reactors were supposed to meet did not materialize. By the summer of 1984 the BPA had a power surplus. Having dramatically raised rates, the BPA offered short-term reduced rates to aluminum smelters struggling in a competitive world industry in which they now paid more for power than did smelters in Canada and Brazil. With a power surplus, the BPA once again needed aluminum customers for revenues to pay off its spiraling debt. It tied the price of the electricity sold to the smelters to world prices for aluminum. By 1991 with dramatic growth in the region, the surplus was gone, and chastened planners faced multiple uncertainties in trying to manage the power supply system.

WPPSS was an astonishing failure, an amazing exercise in irresponsibility. But this was the 1980s, and at certain levels of American society, there was apparently no such thing as responsibility for failure. Donald

Hodel, the head of the BPA, having left the agency in financial shambles and the power system in chaos, went on to become Secretary of Energy in the Reagan administration.

III

When the BPA turned to nuclear power it still turned to the Columbia, for at Hanford the river was already part of one of the largest concentrations of nuclear reactors in the world. WPPSS and the BPA hoped to add new reactors to them and create a nuclear park. Hanford, Senator Warren Magnuson said, "could well become in the years ahead, what the Columbia River system has been for the past thirty years." Its old reactors had produced plutonium for bombs. Its new reactors would produce electricity.

Dams are organic machines that last a long time, but plutonium makes the dams seem as transient as sunlight sparkling on the water. The half-life of plutonium is nearly 25,000 years, and Glenn Seaborg, the physicist who discovered it in 1940, described it as "fiendishly toxic." A "particle the size of an ordinary speck of dust, about 0.6 microgram, constitutes the 'maximum permissible body burden' " in an adult. Manufacturing it creates a stew of less deadly, shorter-lived, but ultimately more troublesome radioactive substances: radioiodine (I-131), radioisotopes of phosphorus (P-32), zinc (Zn-65), chromium (Cr-51), neptunium (Np-239), arsenic (As-76), and many others.

The Hanford Engineer Works, as the Hanford site was originally named, was a "bomb factory." It manufactured plutonium. The Danish physicist Niels Bohr had told American scientists that "to get the fissionable material necessary to make a bomb" they would have to "turn the whole country into a factory." He exaggerated, of course; the factory took up counties not countries. The Hanford Engineer Works became part of an interlocking set of laboratories, manufacturing sites, and testing grounds spread across the nation. The Columbia, too, became part of the factory.

In December 1942, Colonel Franklin Matthias, acting for the Army's Manhattan Project, had chosen a sparsely populated stretch of struggling orchards, farms, and ranches along the Columbia River beginning a few miles north of the mouth of the Yakima River as the site for the manufacture of plutonium. Hanford itself was a small town tainted with failures. It was a failed irrigation project named for and promoted by an impeached federal judge. The town had survived its failures. It would not survive the success of becoming a major government complex. The government bought out and evicted everyone within the reservation, condemning some of the land and leasing the rest.

The government created a new kind of space—an atomic space—on the Columbia. The 670 square miles of reservation that surrounded the complex of reactors and processing plants was half the size of Rhode Island, a state which exists for the West largely as a convenient yardstick to emphasize western vastness and eastern insignificance. But this fractional Rhode Island was tightly bounded and heavily buffered to keep in not only the toxic substances that plutonium production spewed out into the air but the very knowledge of those dangerous substances. Matthias chose Hanford primarily for its isolation. This land, emptied of its inhabitants, would serve as a buffer necessary because of the great but still largely unknown dangers involved in the manufacture of plutonium. Within the reservation the plants were dispersed to "ensure safety against the unknown as well as the known hazards."

The Columbia distinguished this isolated land from similar tracts throughout the West. The Columbia would provide cold, clean water necessary to cool the reactors. The Columbia that produced electricity from the Grand Coulee provided the power for the pumps that drew water up from the river. The river served not only the three original reactors built during the war, but five additional reactors erected during the Cold War construction of 1947–55. For more than a quarter of a century Hanford would produce plutonium.

The Columbia thus ran as part of a giant new machine that created a new source of energy. Plutonium 239 itself was the product of controlled fission. In the piles of the Hanford reactors, the splitting of the uranium atoms produced excess neutrons. Some bombarded other atoms of uranium 235, creating a chain reaction. Others hit rarer atoms of uranium 238, producing plutonium. Some neutrons converted to energy, which appeared as heat. Tons of uranium fuel produced grams of plutonium which had to be chemically separated from the uranium slugs.

This energy served no social purpose. Hanford's eight original graphite-moderated and water-cooled reactors were not designed to produce electricity. Except for a facility to recover enough heat for area buildings, they produced no usable power. The heat the reactors produced was a problem, not an asset. Hanford produced the heat equivalent of 1,500 tons of coal for each pound of plutonium produced. Plutonium production depended on the dissipation of heat.

The cooling system was the limiting factor in production, and the cooling system depended on the river. The first three reactors alone required 30,000 gallons per minute for each pile. Together these three piles required more water than a city of a million people. Originally forty pumps driven by 60,000 kilowatts of Bonneville and Grand Coulee power took water from the river to cool the reactors. Water returned to the river at 74° F.; in 1964 the reactors accounted for most of the 2°–3° F. rise in the temperature of the river between Priest Rapids and Richland during August and September. To Washington politicians, this lost heat became the equivalent of the Columbia flowing unused to the sea. It was a waste. But both private utilities and coal companies bitterly opposed the building of federal reactors that could produce commercial power. Not until 1966, when the multipurpose N-reactor came on line, would a Hanford reactor produce electricity.

Plutonium itself, of course, could produce massive amounts of energy in a nuclear explosion, but only the threat of such an explosion had social utility. If actually detonated, a nuclear bomb not only eliminated the social results of human labor, it eliminated the laborers. That, after all, was its purpose.

Everything at Hanford seemed to produce its opposite, and then blur the distinctions between them. Having chosen the region because of its sparse population, having emptied the original Hanford, the government proceeded to repopulate it. Huge amounts of human labor were necessary to create the organic machine at Hanford. Nell MacGregor, one of the thousands of workers recruited for the project during the war, marveled at the ability not only to construct the plants but to build Hanford itself into a city of more than fifty thousand people complete with a bank, stores, schools, a hospital, and a nursery. Virtually overnight it became the fifth-largest city in the state. And having built the town of Hanford as well as the B, D, and F reactors and the separation facilities in the middle of the desert, the workers, on command in 1945, abandoned and destroyed the town, for it was too close to the reactors to be safe. They had no idea of what they had built or why. It was replaced with an equally planned city, Richland, and with quite unplanned sprawl in the adjoining cities of Pasco and Kennewick. Together they comprised the third most populous region in Washington, one almost totally dependent on federal expenditures. Hanford was both full and empty; populated and depopulated.

Hanford similarly created and then blurred distinctions between the natural and the unnatural. Hanford was a factory producing a product largely unknown in nature, but it was a factory whose danger created space in which nonhuman species could survive. Nell MacGregor was astonished that sand drifts were allowed to fill the doorways of Hanford where thousands had only recently passed. She thought nature had returned. The need for secrecy kept the Hanford Reach undammed. The dangers of its production kept the land around it open, and as a result the reservation became a wildlife oasis. Only here could fall chinooks still spawn in the main channel. Eagles, black-crowned night herons, prairie falcons, long-billed curlews, a profusion of overwintering waterfowl, coyotes, deer, and other species all survived in the shadows of the reactors and processing plants.

But what was natural and what was "unnatural" was precisely what was so confusing about the place. Looking at the abandoned city of Hanford, the journalist Earl Pomeroy saw not a reversion to nature, but a step on the way to "a miracle in the sand and sage—the Hanford Engineer Works, which has wrought something not existing in nature, plutonium."* But what did not previously exist in nature could become a dangerous, constituent part of living things. The very ability of radioactive elements, both those that occurred in nature and those that did not, to combine with living organisms emphasized the links between "nature" and what humans made in an atomic world.

Emerson had long before seen nature in the steam in a boiler, but a nuclear reaction represented a fundamentally new interpenetration of human energy and the energy of nature. Burning oil or coal produces heat; it rearranges intact atoms into new groupings which are then stable. But nuclear fission converts part of the mass of an atom's nucleus into

---

* It actually does exist in minute amounts.

energy. Its consequences go beyond the immediate production of heat. Bombarding stable atoms with neutrons injected an additional neutron into their nuclei; the reactors of Hanford produced over sixty different unstable radionuclides. The chemical separation of plutonium from the fuel rods in the processing plants yielded still more as well as nonradioactive but toxic or carcinogenic chemicals. The radionuclides emit excess energy (radiation) in the form of either an electron (or beta particle), or a neutron, or an alpha particle (two protons and two neutrons). Other types of radioactive materials emit packages of energy— gamma rays, which are physically similar to a ray of light but contain more energy. All forms of radiation are forms of energy, but each has different properties. Alpha rays are not very penetrating, but gamma rays require heavy shielding. Each radionuclide has its own life span (measured as a half-life). Eventually, either in minutes or in millennia, they all decay into a stable form.

Like the river itself, each radionuclide has its own geography, its own pathway which intersects with the flow of water, the movement of air, the circulation of blood. Scientists were initially confident that they could contain the releases of radionuclides, storing the short-lived ones until they were harmless, putting the medium-level wastes into the ground, where they would adsorb or bind with the soil and remain stationary, and holding the most radioactive wastes in storage tanks. They thought that they could prevent damaging amounts of radionuclides from becoming constituent parts of the human body.

But they didn't fully understand the nature of the Hanford Reservation. They soon had to acknowledge the complicated and contrary movement of air which could under certain conditions drive largely undiluted releases from smokestacks back to the ground. They didn't consider adequately the ability of the food chain to concentrate wastes, so that as plants took up nutrients from the soil, as animals ate plants, and as some animals ate other animals, the concentration of radionuclides increased. They were too sanguine about adsorption, not realizing that the ability of the soil to bind wastes through ion exchange depended on the size and shape of the sand and gravel particles and on soil pH. They grossly exceeded their own permissible limits of discharge of effluent into the river during the early race to produce plutonium, and they overestimated the ability of the river to mix and dilute this waste. By 1963 the average release of beta emitters from reactor effluent was around 14,500 curies a day.* It would decline only as the original single-pass reactors were gradually shut down between 1963 and 1971.

These materials, so poorly understood, highlighted the limits of science's understanding of the natural world of the Columbia. Scientists didn't recognize that radionuclides would reach the water table sooner than they predicted. They learned only gradually the complexity of the hydrologic cycle within the table and the way in which the enormous amounts of liquids they dumped (200 billion gallons from the processing plants by 1985) altered and reversed the movements. They didn't realize that the radioactive wastes stored in the tanks on the reservation produced so much heat that the wastes boiled like a toxic witches' brew. And all of these things mattered deeply because large releases into the earth, air, and water—some accidental, some under the rush of production, some as experiments—made that earth, air, and water toxic. Occasional releases of high levels of I-131 continued until 1963, but the largest releases into the air had come during the war and its aftermath. The worst of these was purposeful: the Green Run of 1949. The Green Run followed the successful explosion of the first Soviet atomic bomb. What the AEC sought to test is still classified. But the run put huge amounts of I-131 in the air over a wide area of the Pacific Northwest. At Kennewick readings were 1,000 times the then tolerable limit. Releases into the water table and the river grew as production increased.

When they did recognize what had happened, they obfuscated, they lied, and they deceived. "They" were not some distant power elite, but rather the managers, technicians, and scientists of Richland. It was they who said one thing in secret reports and another thing, or nothing at all, in public, and it was their families as much as an anonymous public that were at risk. They could do this for mundane reasons—it was their job. They justified it for noble reasons. Secrecy was essential. Plutonium guarded American freedom. In the long run, they earnestly believed, atomic bombs saved lives because they acted as a deterrent. With people ignorant of the releases of radiation, there was no fear in the Tri-Cities. As with the salmon, ideologies and ways of life shaped the natural processes of the river. But this time in secret.

---

* A curie is a measure of the amount of radioactive material present based on the number of atoms of an element that decay per second. One curie is 37 billion atoms undergoing decay each second.

For humans, the most interesting parts of these pathways are those which lead to their bodies. Radiation created a new geography of energy on the Columbia. It controlled how people moved within the buildings and on the reservation at Hanford. It controlled how much time could be spent in particular spaces. It influenced how people worked together. Indeed, it is impossible to think seriously about Hanford without recognizing the necessity for the rigorous control of space that radiation imposed. But radiation could not be kept within its assigned space at Hanford. Radioactive materials, some of them versions of innocent materials such as iodine, became part of sagebrush and thistle, of salmon, deer, and human beings. They moved through natural systems.

A particular radioactive geography was created by the intersection of weather, water, soils, plants, animals, markets, specific radionuclides, and our own bodies. The ultimate mapping proceeds on finer and finer levels. Our own physiology does one of the final sortings. The thyroid gathers up iodine 131. Arsenic 76, chromium 51, copper 64, and neptunium 239 gravitate to the lower large intestine. Manganese 56 goes to the upper large intestine, phosphorus 32 to bone marrow, sodium 24 to the bone surface in particular and the whole body in general; zinc 65, too, goes to the whole body. The effects of radiation varied with the material. In some cases the energy that caused biological effects came from the carrier, but in others the energy was released from the tissue itself by the trigger action of nuclear reactions.

Iodine 131 created perhaps the most studied and complicated geography, the map of which is still tentative as dose reconstruction projects proceed. Hanford separation plants released more than 685,000 curies of iodine 131 during its first three years of operation. Approximately 3,000 people received an 840-rad dose to their thyroids. An 840-rad dose is 70 times the average annual exposure from natural causes.* Some of that radiation reached the thyroids of infants, who are far more vulnerable to such radiation than adults. Whether iodine 131 took this pathway depended on the type of emissions, the weather conditions at the time of release, the season, the growth of forage, the location of cows that ate the forage, the market distribution of milk from those cows, and the distribution of infants in the area where the milk was consumed. It was a doubly invisible geography: first, because

* A rad is a measurement of energy deposited by radiation in the body.

those who lived within it did not know the routes by which iodine 131 entered the human body (and most did not even know that iodine 131 existed at all), and second, because those who knew about the emissions purposefully kept them secret. But it was a quite real geography.

When iodine 131 concentrates in the human thyroid, it can emit enough energy to begin destroying the surrounding tissue. Current studies, however, can speak only in terms of probabilities. We can't say exactly where iodine 131 went or whose thyroids contained it. But we do know that the movement of iodine 131 through space, the spatial organization of markets, and the spaces people occupied intersected to help determine who would live and who would die.

There is little doubt these releases killed people. But we can never know with certainty who was killed; whose cancer was natural and whose was not. These deaths were planned because the releases were planned, although the planners never intended to kill individual victims. They acted for a greater good.

sounds funny to say "natural" after all this.

Seen in one way, Hanford represented a transcendence of nature. It produced elements unknown in nature. It promised energy free from the limits of wind, water, and the stored solar energy of oil and coal. Seen another way, Hanford only complicated natural systems. It could not escape the movement of wind and water or the life cycles of plants and animals. It could not escape human bodies. It became another complicating and dangerous element in a vastly complicated organic machine.

Huge amounts of human labor and the wealth it produced went into creating Hanford. Even more labor and wealth will go into cleaning it up, or, more accurately, into confining the waste. Estimates of the total cost of the first five years of the cleanup are $3.1 billion. The total cost could exceed $50 billion. WPPSS and Hanford showed that the organic machine could consume as well as produce enormous amounts of wealth. The work that goes on at Hanford, like the work on the dams, brings a knowledge of nature. But this is a knowledge that comes from unbuilding what earlier labor had built.

CHAPTER 4
Salmon

I

In the beginning it had been salmon that had drawn humans to the river. The places where the river's energy was greatest—at the Dalles and the Cascades, and Celilo Falls, at Kettle Falls and Priest Rapids— had concentrated the salmon when they returned to spawn, and at these places fishermen, too, concentrated. The energy harvested and stored by salmon for their journey had become calories that supported human life along the river. Salmon had knit together the energy of land and sea; they had knit together human and nonhuman labor; salmon had defined the river for millennia.

By the 1930s, that decade of crises, there was a widespread conviction that "a crisis confronts the salmon fisheries, particularly the Columbia River." Huge areas of spawning grounds had vanished; the catches had already declined by 50 percent of their 1911 peak. And now the Grand Coulee Dam, rising on the Columbia, would seal off the upper Columbia, closing it to salmon. Adding the area lost to the Grand Coulee Dam to existing losses meant that 70 percent of the original spawning area of Columbia River salmon would be gone.

Fishermen and biologists feared the dams, but they also knew that preserving the runs involved more than allowing sufficient spawners to proceed upstream. Even dams equipped with fishways, and thus passable by returning adults, might kill young salmon trying to reach the sea. And dams were only one entry in a quite sophisticated catalogue of dangers. Irrigation agriculture killed salmon with its unscreened ditches and diversion dams. Stock raising brought erosion and destruction of riparian habitats. Lumbering, too, increased erosion, blocked streams, and, by eliminating shade, raised water temperature. Cities and industries polluted the rivers. Virtually the full modern list of environmental hazards to salmon was known and publicized even though the actual life history and ecology of salmon remained poorly understood.

Our knowledge of the dangers we pose to salmon is now half a century old; our knowledge has ultimately made little difference. Far from being eliminated, the dangers have multiplied. Today, the Columbia River system is no longer particularly suitable for salmon. What was once cool water has become warm; what was fast water has become stilled; what was clean has become fouled; what was reasonably free of predators of young salmon has become full of them. The list could go on and on. Fewer and fewer salmon pass up the river; the vast majority of smolts never reach the sea. The end result, as far as wild salmon are concerned, is that what was once abundant has become scarce.

That's what Sue says →

Yet standing by the fish ladder at Ice Harbor, the first dam on the Snake River, on a hot July afternoon in 1994, I see fish everywhere. There are large carp and schools of shad, neither native to the river, but only a few chinook, no sockeye, and only a scattering of steelhead. The river has changed. To say that there should be thousands of chinook and sockeye passing upriver on a given day in early July instead of the nineteen chinook of July 11, 1994, is, perhaps, to miss the point. If this were the old Columbia River system there should be salmon, but this is a different river. It is not the river salmon evolved in. This new river produces carp and shad.

The architects of the new river have been nearly constant in their protestations of concern for salmon, but they have quite consciously made a choice against the conditions that produce salmon. They have wanted the river and its watershed to say electricity, lumber, cattle, and fruit and together these have translated into carp, shad, and squawfish instead of salmon. If ever a death could be unintended and overdetermined, it is the death of the wild runs of the Columbia River salmon.

But paradoxically, even in their decline, salmon remain culturally as powerful as when they passed upriver in a flood of abundant life. They are repositories of meaning. People still desire salmon. Salmon symbolize nature in the Pacific Northwest; the experience of taking them has become a quintessential Northwest experience. Salmon are not just fish on the Columbia; they are tokens of a way of life.

Claims to salmon are so passionately made and defended because they are more than economic. Economics can make no sense of Columbia River salmon. We now spend far more in saving them than we do in catching them. It is an investment that will probably never yield an economic return. Nor do Indians, gillnetters, and sportsmen take salmon primarily for the money the fish yields. They fish because the act of catching salmon partially defines who they are and the lives they wish to lead. When in 1952 the Yakima tribal council protested the drowning of Celilo Falls by the Dalles Dam, council members emphasized how the loss would cut deep into Yakima customary and religious practices. These practices have changed considerably over the last two centuries, but salmon remain central to them.

As a cultural talisman, wild salmon have demonstrated their power as they have diminished in numbers. Scarce salmon have pitted fishers against one another in recurring "fish fights" along the Columbia. They have sparked expensive efforts to replace wild salmon with hatchery salmon. They have sparked an unsuccessful opposition to the dams whose electricity replaced the salmon as the great good that the river could offer. They briefly made nuclear energy an environmental savior; reactors, by eliminating the need for dams, would preserve the salmon. But reactors, by warming the river, increased mortality in salmon. And now, with more runs dwindling to extinction, the decline of salmon has sparked a widespread environmental offensive against the dams, against ranching, against irrigation farming, against logging, against all the activities along the river that threaten the fish. The economic value of the Columbia salmon has not been much of an indicator of its cultural power.

Such battles over salmon are not new. Salmon and steelhead have, as Courtland Smith has pointed out, always been "our fish." There is always a "they" who must be prevented from taking "our fish." As salmon runs reached a point of crisis in the 1930s, fights over access to the fish erupted. Salmon fishing is, and long has been, political; it is ideological. It is about staking a defensible social claim to a share of the catch and calling that claim a defense of nature: the fewer the fish, the more intense the fight.

Resolutions of that fight have had little to do with economic efficiency. The most economically efficient fishers were the first to lose
access to the fishery. In both Oregon and Washington in the 1920s and
1930s a combination of popular ballot initiatives and legislative acts
eliminated traps, fish wheels, and seines from the river. On the whole,
it has been sportsmen, the most economically inefficient fishers, who
have made the greatest gains. In 1980, Peter Larkin, a noted fisheries
expert, pointed out that sportfishing is about *inefficiency*. The goal is
to have as many people as possible devote as much time as possible and
spend as much money as possible for devices that will never pay for
themselves in terms of fish caught. For sportsmen the labor of catching
fish has become a form of leisure, an escape from work that mimics
work, a reattachment to nature that resembles Kipling's search for chinooks. Salmon are not so much a means of making a good living as
symbols of the good life itself.

II

Dams are at the heart of the declining salmon runs, but a dam is
not inherently harmful to salmon; their placement and operation
do matter. Properly located and managed, a dam can in some situations
help salmon. Upriver of the spawning grounds, it can prevent losses
associated with flood or drought by regulating flow. By acting as a
settlement basin, it can remove silt and with it a major cause of mortality
in salmon eggs downstream. A dam raises water temperature at the
surface of its pool, but if it releases cold water from the depth of its
reservoir, it can keep summer river temperatures cool and favorable.

But the dams built on the Columbia River and its tributaries were
not designed with salmon in mind. Sitting astride the migration routes
of a large proportion of Columbia River salmon and flooding spawning
sites, they posed a danger to the continuation of the runs. And by posing
a threat to fish, they posed a danger to all fishers on the river. This
common danger forced occasional truces in the battles between Indians,
sportsmen, and commercial fishers for a greater share of the catch. A
common enemy forced them, along with biologists and fishery managers, into a shaky and uneasy alliance to save the fishery itself.

Fishery interests possessed the foresight to recognize that the critical fights over Columbia salmon would take place around authorization of the new dams to be built after the Bonneville and the Grand Coulee. The fights over McNary, the Dalles, and the lower Snake River dams in many ways decided the fate of the fishery. The advocates of the fishery, however, were not an imposing force. Historically, they have been weak and divided; their opponents have been strong and united. And since overfishing, particularly commercial overfishing, has played a role in depleting the runs, fishing interests came to the table with dirty hands. Supporters of the dams could turn the fishers' own evidence of depletion into a demand for the cessation of commercial fishing.

Nor did the site of the battle favor the fishers. The war over salmon has been and continues to be fought in bureaucracies and the halls of Congress. Fishery interests needed strong allies, but they were teamed with bureaucratic weaklings while power, irrigation, and navigation interests had bureaucratic bruisers on their side. Responsibility for Columbia salmon in the immediate postwar years fell largely to the Washington Department of Fisheries, the Oregon Fish Commission, the U.S. Fish and Wildlife Service, and the Bureau of Indian Affairs. They were no match for the Army Corps of Engineers, the Bureau of Reclamation, and the BPA.

And as if all these difficulties were not enough, the mystique of salmon, its noneconomic value, was initially diluted by its very abundance. Salmon had declined, but they had, ironically, not declined enough to excite widespread *public* alarm. In the 1930s, W. H. Rich, Director of Research for the Oregon Fish Commissioner, argued that the salmon were worthy of "consideration far beyond their immediate economic value," but his pleas largely went unheeded. The meaning of the salmon remained opaque, scattered among many scaly bodies; it became clear only as it became concentrated in the fewer and fewer salmon who remained. This would take years. And in the meantime, fishery interests took another stance. They made the fishery seem a purely technical problem in a largely economic enterprise. Managers, canners, and commercial fishermen defined salmon as "capital." Columbia salmon in 1940 yielded about $10 million. This represented a 4 percent return on a $250 million investment. Salmon became $250 million of swimming capital. Such commodification of the salmon seemed hardheaded and realistic. In fact, it made little sense. It put salmon into an economic contest it could never win. For what if agriculture was more valuable? Or cattle and sheep? Or logging? Or hydroelectricity? Or what if the cost of saving Columbia salmon exceeded the value of the fishery (as it now does)? If we have to choose, should salmon then surrender the river for more profitable uses? By the 1950s there was public controversy over whether the fishery was worth the cost.

The most immediate problem faced by those seeking to save salmon in the 1940s now seems the most unlikely: they had to prove that the new dams would, in fact, harm salmon. They were convinced that each additional dam did not just add a new increment of loss but increased losses as a geometric function. The first dam weakened fish; additional dams took an even greater toll. If one dam caused a 5 percent loss, three dams would cause far more than a 15 percent loss.

Such concerns about the consequences of additional dams were essentially correct. Salmon always have expended energy to travel upstream, but the dams altered how and when they expended their energy. By the 1950s scientists were discovering that Columbia River sockeye, which before the dams had gradually lost muscle fat during their migration, now suffered a drastic loss at the Bonneville Dam. More dams meant greater problems. By the late 1980s estimates of upstream mortality averaged 5 to 10 percent of the migrants at each dam. Cumulative mortalities for nine dams on the Columbia and Snake amounted to 37 to 61 percent of the total run. Such losses would, as it turned out, be scant compared to losses of downstream migrants.

In the 1940s biologists had deep suspicions but only ambiguous evidence of the harm dams would cause. Initially, neither the Bonneville nor the Grand Coulee appeared to harm the fishery irreparably. To laypeople, congressional committees, and some scientists and managers, the Bonneville and the Grand Coulee seemed to prove the opposite: fishing could exist alongside energy, irrigation, and transportation.

A folklore has grown up about the Bonneville that, as originally designed, the dam contained no fishways. But except for artists' sketches, there were always provisions for fish passage at the Bonneville; the battle was over fish locks versus fishways, and then the adequacy and cost of the fishways. Both were eventually built; indeed, the *Pacific Fisherman* thought the design incorporated "fishways . . . vaster than will prove necessary."

When the returning runs passed over the ladders, the popular press and the Columbia Basin Interagency Committee (CBIAC, whose Fisheries Steering Committee along with the Pacific Northwest Coordination Committee would help set salmon policy in the 1940s) acclaimed them a great success. And in 1946, Frank Bell, a former U.S. Commissioner of Fisheries and a vice president of the Columbia River Development League, testified that turbines at the Bonneville Dam only left the smolts passing downstream "groggy." Only in 1952, when later dams had been authorized and were under construction, did studies indicate that on average 10 to 15 percent of all the smolts passing the Bonneville Dam died there. In the worst years up to half the smolts may have been lost. Dam building raced ahead of knowledge of the consequences of the dams.

Although it blocked access to 1,100 miles of spawning grounds, the Grand Coulee also did not seem an unmitigated disaster for the fisheries. Engineers thought it technically possible to elevate adults over the dam, but regarded the effort as pointless because there was no way to pass smolts downstream over or through the massive structure. Fishery interests had neither the power nor the desire to stop the dam; they settled for compensatory measures. Agriculture and aquiculture could supposedly exist side by side.

Biologists undertook a fish relocation project. They found a new home for salmon on tributaries below the dam where irrigation had previously depleted or destroyed salmon runs. They built an expensive new hatchery at Leavenworth Station on Icicle Creek to supplement the relocated runs. And, finally, they began screening irrigation ditches and regulating flow to diminish losses elsewhere in the system.

Such efforts involved dramatic and intrusive mechanical interventions. Fish that spawned above the Grand Coulee were trapped at the Rock Island Dam and carried in specially designed fish trucks to Icicle Creek. They were held in ponds designed "to duplicate as nearly as possible a natural environment." When their eggs ripened, they were artificially spawned. Their bodies were dehydrated, ground up, and fed to their own young. These fingerlings were reared at Icicle Creek and three other auxiliary hatcheries before being released into the Wenatchee, Okanogan, Entiat, and Methow river systems.

After a shaky start, the results seemed promising. A 1948 study concluded that despite substantial problems at the Leavenworth hatchery (which never operated close to its 40-million-egg capacity), the relocation of salmon and steelhead succeeded beyond expectations. The Grand Coulee Fish Maintenance Project diverted hatchery-raised descendants of upriver runs of spring and summer chinook and sockeyes into the river systems between the Rock Island and Grand Coulee dams. The U.S. Fish and Wildlife Service admitted that many of the conditions that had eliminated the original runs in these rivers still remained, and that additional dams would increase the dangers, but corrective measures had been taken and long-term rehabilitation appeared "possible but difficult."

Faced with such seeming success and not wanting to be seen as obstacles to development, fishermen, canners, and many biologists were left to play oddly amenable Cassandras on the Columbia. They prophesied doom and made deals with various Panglosses on congressional committees and the power agencies. They cited specific horror stories about the Army Corps of Engineers, who on the Willamette continued to locate dams with a criminal neglect of their impact on salmon. They predicted worse damage to come. In 1946 the Fish and Wildlife Service declared that the McNary Dam alone might eventually result in the extermination of all the salmon passing the site. Construction of all the proposed Columbia and Snake River dams "would literally destroy the valuable Columbia River salmon fishery."

And then, despite their own dire warnings, fishing interests tried to be accommodating to development. They offered fantasies of nuclear power eliminating the need for dams. They tried to draw a line between necessary and unnecessary dams. But in venturing into the economics of energy, they played into the BPA's hands. The BPA existed not just to supply electricity but to stimulate a demand for it. There could never be enough dams. The fishing interests retreated to asking that additional dams be built only where there were no substantial fish runs. The BPA rejected this as impossible. If dams must interfere with existing runs, the fishers asked for a ten-year delay to figure out how to save the runs. And finally, having failed to defeat or delay the dams, they demanded compensation through new hatcheries and removal of other existing hazards to salmon. And this the BPA was willing to consent to and Congress was willing to grant. T. F. Sandoz, the secretary of the Columbia Basin Fisheries Development Association, argued that it was useless to appropriate millions to save the fish while hundreds of millions were appropriated for the dams to destroy them. But essentially, this was what would be done.

The Bonneville and the Grand Coulee, viewed in one light as disasters for salmon, became from another angle the models for rehabilitating the fisheries. A program of fishways similar to those at the Bonneville, coupled with stream rehabilitation and hatcheries like those at the Grand Coulee, would supposedly compensate for what dams destroyed. Vast sums were spent. The fisheries development program first funded in 1949 had spent $84 million on mitigation by 1975; when fishways and state and private spending were added, the total came to $400 million. This was just the beginning. Between 1981 and 1991 salmon protection costs reached $1.34 billion.

Since mitigation focused largely on hatcheries and restricting damage from overfishing, pollution, lumbering, ranching, and logging, it was easy to think of these as the main problems confronting the fishery. This would become a standard BPA position. Managing fish has meant compensating for damage, not preventing it. It has meant hatcheries instead of spawning grounds; rehabilitating old rivers to replace rivers blocked by dams; barging smolts downstream to replace the current that once flushed them to the sea. It has meant regulating and allocating the catch to try to both maximize production and ensure that enough spawners returned to propagate new runs.

Unfortunately, the program of mitigation and rehabilitation has not worked. The Columbia has numerous kinds and runs of salmon and not all runs have declined at the same pace. There are yearly variations. There are temporary recoveries for some species and runs, but overall the decline has been pervasive and general. The catches on the Columbia are one measure of the decline. From 1880 to 1930 the catch was 33.9 million pounds a year. From 1931 to 1948 it declined to 23.8 million. From 1949 to 1973 the yearly average fell to 10.9 million pounds. In 1993 the catch was 1.4 million pounds.

This decline has taken place despite intensive management. If anything, there have been too many managers. There is no fisheries equivalent of the BPA with responsibility for the fishery as a whole. The fish pass through numerous jurisdictions; what happens in one area negates efforts in another. And not all the threats to salmon are under the potential control of any management scheme. There continue to be natural systems operating without human control.

When salmon leave the river, they migrate into the Pacific, where patterns of energy production, of scarcity and abundance, have been poorly known and beyond human control. The power of El Niño events changed wind and weather patterns, and altered ocean currents, temperature, and salinity. It reduced the upwelling of deeper waters, suppressed necessary food supplies, and brought to the northern Pacific coast new fish that competed with and preyed on salmon. In 1982–83, El Niño devastated the salmon fishery, killing, for example, an estimated half of the adult coho that would have normally returned to spawn. The El Niño of 1993–94 has had similar effects.

The failure to stabilize the runs has inevitably meant more pressure on the fishery. The temporary truces among fishers and the fragile alliance of fishers against the dams have failed to hold. As dams rearranged the rivers, new fish fights rearranged the allocation of the catch. Sportsmen became the predominant, and the most aggressive, group in the Columbia River fishery. With sponsors in the Oregon Fish Commission and the Washington Department of Fisheries, sportfishers have tried to increase their share of the fish by eliminating or restricting both gillnetters and Indian fishers. An initiative measure in Oregon to ban gillnetters failed, but Washington and Oregon curtailed commercial fishing seasons on the river to ensure that enough spawners passed upriver to continue the runs. The 1,192 gillnetters fishing in 1938, for example, had a 272-day fishing season. The 1,104 gillnetters of 1973 had 73 fishing days. The commercial fishery for spring and summer chinook and sockeye virtually vanished in the early 1970s, and the remaining fisheries showed an alarming decline. In 1993 there were 10 fishing days on the Columbia. In 1994 there were none.

The decline of gillnetters has not meant an elimination of commercial fishing. As regulations tightened on the Columbia and as markets for fresh, frozen, and mild-cured fish expanded, many gillnetters had become, at least seasonally, ocean trollers. By the 1960s trollers emerged as the most productive commercial salmon fishermen. Charter boats also carried sportsmen to sea. The total catch on the Columbia River ceased to be an accurate gauge of the productivity of the fishery because so many immature salmon were caught before they ever returned to the Columbia. Trollers and sportsmen took salmon virtually year-round, but, in doing so, they left nature's work incomplete: From the coasts of Alaska to northern California they took Columbia salmon that had not attained full growth. Their inefficiency extended beyond this. Where once the drift of the current had provided the energy necessary to take fish, now boats burned expensive fuel to go to sea and drag hooks.

Trollers, in turn, eventually faced competition from foreign fishing vessels, particularly the Soviets, who appeared off Washington and Oregon in 1965. Although often bitterly divided among themselves, all American fishers knew salmon didn't belong to foreigners. The United States Fisheries Conservation and Management Act of 1976, which extended national jurisdiction to 200 miles, drove them off. But to the trollers' dismay, the act created new mechanisms for restricting their catch and redistributing the catch toward fishermen on the river.

Indian fishermen, too, participated in the bruising fish fights of mid-century. During the 1930s they had been unintended beneficiaries of battles between whites. Although promoted as a conservation measure, the elimination of fixed gear increased the Indian catch by removing the fish wheels that had narrowed Indian access to their ancient fishing sites. Indians tripled their share of the commercial catch of chinooks on the river to 9 percent between 1935 and 1939. Their success made them the bête noire of sportsmen, gillnetters, and state fish and game departments. Salmon ran a gauntlet of fishers from Alaska to their spawning grounds, and the relative few who made it to the Cascades, whites argued, were needed to restore the runs. Indians, whose major fishing sites began at the Cascades, were thus the designated conservationists, bearing the burden of conservation for runs whites had depleted.

Indians fought back, and their major weapons were the treaties of 1855. In exchange for vast cessions of land, they had preserved their access to the fisheries. They could not ban whites from these fisheries—fishing took place in common with whites—but, the Indians contended, neither could whites restrict their access to these usual and accustomed fishing places. And on this ground the Indians fought in the federal and state bureaucracies, in Congress, and in the courts. They have had to fight for most of the twentieth century. They had preserved access to the fishing sites in earlier court cases, but this was insufficient. The states, the tribes contended, had no right to regulate them at all. The dams created a new issue, for they threatened to make the controversy of state regulation at the Indians' usual and accustomed places moot by eliminating the usual and accustomed places.

Indians faced not only restrictions by the states, which continued to assert their right to regulate Indian fishing despite the treaties, but also the physical elimination of their fishing sites. The Indian dip-net fisheries were small and intimately known places. "All these usual custom fishing places and rocks have names and I know all of them," Tommy Thompson, the eighty-year-old leader of Celilo village wrote the congressional Committee on Indian Affairs in 1945. When dip-netting sites disappeared, sites that concentrated human memories as much as fish, sites that united lineages and families in labor, sites that were valued and ancient possessions, also vanished beneath the water. The Bonneville Dam had destroyed the Indian dip-net fishery at the Cascades. The Grand Coulee had drowned the dip-net fishery at Kettle Falls.

The Dalles Dam doomed the last-remaining Columbia dip-net fishery at Celilo Falls, where roughly 2,000 Indians still fished. The dam, as the federal agencies privately admitted, clearly violated treaty promises. The Yakimas, Umatillas, the people of the Warm Springs reservation, and the residents of Celilo village all knew the treaties gave them the right to fish at their usual and accustomed places. Over tribal and Bureau of Indian Affairs protests, however, the dam went forward. The Army Corps of Engineers evaluated the fishery, assigned a monetary value to the difference between the destroyed sites and alternative sites where Indians could work their fisheries, and paid the Indians $27.2 million in damages. The CBIAC recommended that the BIA develop "alternative economic opportunities" for displaced fishermen. By 1957 a place where human work had created a knowledge of the river, where work had defined a way of life, a place that was already ancient when Lewis and Clark had passed, existed no more.

In the distorted and divisive fish politics of the Columbia, the destruction of Celilo Falls became a conservation measure. Brigadier General C. H. Chorpening of the Army Corps of Engineers explained that state agencies and conservationists thought the "continuation of commercial fishing above the Bonneville Dam endangers the entire resource." Eliminating Indian fishing "through construction of the

Dalles Dam, accordingly, would be a continuing direct and outstanding contribution toward conservation of the fishery resources in the Columbia River Basin."

The Indians, however, did not consent to this latest effort to remove them for the greater good. Their catch fell precipitously in the 1950s, but they replaced their dip-net fishery with a gill-net fishery and restored catch levels to just below the dip-net totals of the late 1940s. They fought additional attempts to remove them, and court decisions in the 1970s guaranteed their treaty rights to preferential access to the resource. As commercial harvests were restricted downstream, their percentage of the total harvest rose from under 1 percent in 1960 to 35 percent in 1974. In 1974 the decision of Judge Boldt ruling in related Indian treaties gave them a 50 percent share of the runs. The Indians' share of the runs increased, but the runs continued to decline.

The rehabilitation program that took place alongside dam construction did achieve some success. Hatchery production improved in the 1950s, and there was a period of optimism for some species. When adjusted for catches of immature salmon at sea, the Columbia *as a whole* between 1969 and 1973 was still producing an estimated 90 percent of the 1880–1930 average catch despite dramatically reduced spawning areas. But a closer look revealed that both the commercial fishery and the fish were in trouble. In hindsight it may have been abnormally good ocean conditions, not human efforts, that maintained the fishery in the 1960s. And because of ocean trolling and sportfishing, a much smaller percentage of the commercial catch was on the Columbia itself. As fewer fish reached the Columbia, a higher percentage had to be reserved for spawning.

Despite dramatic restrictions on fishing in the river, however, the runs began to decline. This puzzled fish biologists because the restrictions did secure an adequate passage of upriver spawners. In the late 1960s counts of salmon passing the Rock Island Dam were higher than at any time since counts began in 1933. Why, then, were so few fish returning in the 1970s?

The problem didn't seem to be the production of smolts. The spawning grounds were suffering, but hatcheries were turning out more fish. They would account for half the runs on the Columbia by 1979. But returns of hatchery fish were also falling. By the late 1960s increases in hatchery production did not yield increases in the fishery. Studies did show the Columbia coho runs to be increasing, but virtually all the other runs were in decline.

The trouble, fishery experts suspected, was the increasing failure of the juvenile salmon to reach the sea. In 1965, Oregon Fish Commission studies recognized that *"a mounting volume of evidence has pointed to failure of the downstream migrations as the major cause of the vanishing runs."* Immature salmon do not swim downstream. They leave their home streams tail-first; the current washes them toward the sea. But in the reservoirs of dams there was no current to speak of. Their journey lengthened; they became more vulnerable to disease and to predators such as squawfish which multiplied in the reservoirs. And each dam presented a threat. To go through the turbines meant death, but being washed over the spillway also often meant death. In the 1970s scientists connected high mortality among juvenile salmon migrating to the sea with gas-bubble disease, caused when water going over high dams became supersaturated with nitrogen. Nitrogen supersaturation levels above 105 percent produced symptoms of gas-bubble disease, weakening the fish; concentrations above 120 percent were lethal. Given the lack of storage capacity on the river in the early 1970s, such spills were routine during peak spring and summer runoff. In a normal river flow supersaturated water would mix with other water and return to equilibrium, but this did not happen in the Columbia, where each reservoir extended to the dam above it. Instead, nitrogen levels often tended to rise at each successive dam. Coho could still increase because they largely spawned below the Bonneville Dam. The Environmental Protection Agency predicted a 90 percent reduction in salmon runs above the Bonneville Dam within three years if nothing was done to curtail or compensate for the spills.

High dams and nitrogen supersaturation set the stage for the current crisis. Depending on the volume and timing of streamflows, estimates of the cumulative mortality of fish migrating downstream past nine dams ranged from 77 to 96 percent. To escape the choice between sending juvenile salmon through turbines and spilling them over the top, the BPA, with the EPA's blessing, began first trucking and then barging fish downstream. Barging allowed large hatchery releases to be coordinated with skimming and transport operations at the dams. The desire to preserve salmon was changing the early life of a salmon almost beyond recognition. Born in a hatchery, skimmed up at a dam, transported downriver in a barge, a salmon faced the sea.

Hatchery fish were, biologists largely agreed, inferior fish. They appeared to be "less well adapted to the extremes of freshwater and saltwater environment than wild fish," less able to cope with predators, and less hardy. Hatcheries lessened the genetic diversity of the species and were more vulnerable to disease. But despite their deficiencies hatchery fish had a huge advantage in the managed fishery. The majority of hatchery fish were originally raised and released on the lower river below the dams. Wild fish and hatchery fish mingled on their return to the Columbia. When faced with a heavy run, managers, concerned only about the return of hatchery fish, let a set number of spawners pass and then allowed heavy fishing below the dams. Taking 90 percent of 10,000 fish returning to a hatchery was the mark of a successful fishery, but the harvest of 90 percent of a marginal natural run of 100 fish could mean the end of the run. By 1979 an Environmental Impact Study prepared for the Army Corps of Engineers matter-of-factly stated that while natural runs below the Bonneville Dam might survive, "mortality of mid-Columbia runs continues at a level which probably precludes the survival of natural (wild) stocks."

In 1980, the same year the last Columbia cannery shut down, the Pacific Northwest Electric Power Planning and Conservation Act mandated that the Northwest Power Planning Council take measures to enhance fish and wildlife while assuring the Northwest of an adequate and efficient power supply. The Council, estimating that hydropower had diminished the salmon and steelhead runs by 5 to 11 million fish annually, sought to double the then current run size of 2.5 million fish. They gave priority to the runs above the Bonneville Dam. And for the first time, they tried to change the operation of the river rather than just mitigate the effects of management. Their plans regulated flows to help push salmon downstream and some dams were retrofitted with juvenile bypass systems to keep smolts out of the turbines. But given the gravity of the situation, the changes were modest; they failed to achieve their goals.

The clock was ticking and nature speeded it up, reminding us that it was not only humans that influenced the salmon. El Niño in the early 1980s and early 1990s, and drought beginning in 1986, hit the runs hard. On the crucial Snake River the wild stocks fell drastically after 1978, with only sporadic and moderate upward fluctuations. By the 1990s it was becoming apparent that many of the remaining wild runs of Columbia salmon might dwindle out with the century. In 1991 several runs of Snake River salmon were given protection under the Endangered Species Act.

The Snake River sockeye composed one of those runs. Their last remaining spawning ground is Redfish Lake in Idaho. Redfish Lake is a spectacular place. Its waters back up against the aptly named Sawtooth Mountains; it is a fitting end for an epic journey. Averaging thirteen miles a day, the sockeye swim nine hundred miles up the Columbia to the Snake, up the Snake to the Salmon, and then up the Salmon to Redfish Creek and Redfish Lake. As they wait to spawn, their bodies turn red; they spawn and die.

But few return anymore. In 1955 nearly 4,500 fish had returned; between zero and eight sockeye salmon have returned to the lake each year since 1990. The problem is not in the ocean, nor are sockeye per se in danger of extinction. On the Fraser River in Canada half a million sockeye returned in 1993. The total Fraser sockeye run numbered over 20 million fish.

The Snake River sockeye have acquired that most dangerous of human cultural signs: the survivors have individual names, like pets, like domestic animals, like the last passenger pigeon. In 1991 the one female that returned to Redfish Lake was named Sally. In Sally the sockeye's case, however, human sentimentality did not divert her from her appointed end: like any hatchery fish, when ripe, she was killed and stripped of her eggs.

Sally's fate underlines the ironies of saving endangered "natural" runs. The Columbia has become an organic machine, and the definition of wild and natural has blurred for the species that live in it. Sally's descendants are not obviously wild; they are part of a captive breeding program. The smolts in the net pens have a mixed ancestry: some are from wild sockeye like Sally, others from combinations of wild sockeye crossed with fish captured while leaving the lake and raised in captivity. The smolts are kept in net pens in the lake. They are released into the lake, overwinter there, and then head downstream in the spring. Some of them will be caught again at the lake's outlet to continue the captive breeding program. Those that do escape will, if they are to survive, be gathered at the Snake River dams and barged downstream. At every phase of their life they are subject to human intervention and oversight. They are less a wild species than a swimming genetic bank.

The politics and science of this frantic management are desperate, hostile, and occasionally crazed. Old enemies have become new allies; claims of environmental sensitivity have emerged in the most unlikely places. There have been moments for the cynical to savor. In February 1994, Kenneth Peterson, president of Columbia Aluminum, filed suit to protect the salmon. He wanted to stop the "squandering of the inheritance of our children." For half a century the turbines that ground smolts to fish meal had sent their electricity to the aluminum industry. The aluminum industry has bitterly opposed any management of the river that deflected the Columbia from its duty to provide electrical energy. When it comes to dams, Mr. Peterson managed to keep his solicitude for the salmon under control. It was the gillnetters he sued, not the BPA.

Kenneth Peterson blames the gillnetters; then-Congressman Tom Foley blamed evolution. After a Foley speech in eastern Washington in April 1992, the *Seattle Post-Intelligencer* reported that an elderly farmer walked up and handed Foley a can of Alaska salmon. "Endangered species, you can go to the store and buy it anytime," said Walt Schweiger. "Alaska is one of our states. Why worry about Washington and Oregon [salmon]?"

Foley essentially agreed. "We should," he said, "take a very, very careful look at the Endangered Species Act before Congress reauthorizes it." The speaker argued that the act "turns a blind eye to the cost" of preservation measures. He warned that some measures could be so extreme as to do "tremendous economic harm to a whole series of communities." "The whole history of evolution, as I know it, is of the creation and destruction of species," said Foley. Leaving aside this "evolutionary" logic (which seems the equivalent of using the inevitability of death to justify murder), Mr. Foley turns a politically profitable blind eye to the considerable subsidies that have gone to both irrigation farming and hydroelectric dams.

Salmon politics have even emerged in an odd form at Hanford. Radioactive wastes in Hanford's water table still move slowly and inexorably toward the Columbia, but aboveground the cooling ponds that once held contaminated water while short-lived isotopes decayed now hold salmon. The Yakima Nation has turned some of the ponds into salmon hatcheries.

Science is at once the supposed referee in all these quarrels and the authority sought for justifying the death or ensuring the resurrection of salmon. But science on the Columbia breaks down quickly into quarreling scientists. Bill Rudolph of the *Alaska Fisherman's Journal* is one of the most perceptive and caustic observers of this latest round of fish fights. Rudolph has noted that the public pressure on scientists to fix the river and their own dependence on funding from the various principals in the controversy have turned much of the public science into little more than "sophisticated name calling."

Still, it is hard not to sympathize with the scientists. They are largely honorable people disdainful of the idea that their funders can buy their conclusions. Nothing so crass happens. But what does happen, inevitably, is that funders prefer to bankroll the research that seems to support their own interests. This is particularly true of the computer models that will probably decide the fate of the Snake River salmon. The real contribution of science has been to shift the arena of the argument from the actual river to a virtual river.

In a very real sense the Columbia has taken the logical step beyond being an organic machine. It has become a virtual river. In the virtual Columbia electronic fish swim past electronic dams on video terminals. Change the electronic river and the fate of the electronic fish is graphically displayed. But this oversimplifies. There are really two virtual rivers. One is FLUSH (Fish Leaving Under Several Hypotheses), a model biologists created for the Columbia River Inter-Tribal Fish Commission. The BPA has funded a second, more expensive and sophisticated model: CRiSP (Columbia River Salmon Passage). The virtual salmon in these models are supposed to mimic actual salmon in the river, but the extent to which this is true remains to be seen. And in a very real sense, this is no longer the issue. The virtual river influences events in the actual Columbia. How electronic fish behave will lead to decisions on how fish in the actual Columbia—the organic machine —will be managed. That the various virtual Columbias depend on the actual Columbia for some of their own electrical power only compounds the ironies and connections.

These models are playing a major role in yet another attempt to find a management plan for the river that will accommodate wild salmon and steelhead. In what is still an ongoing process (which has already found itself in the courts), the BPA, the Army Corps of Engineers, and the Bureau of Reclamation began a System Operation Review (SOR), screening various operating options. The options are wide-ranging; one includes drastic alterations in the dams so that the flow would simulate a natural river for part of the year. The Columbia, in effect, would become a mimetic river, seasonally imitating its old self.

But this is not the option which has engaged the modelers. The models agree on much. There is a need for a wide range of reforms— essentially the same reforms urged since the 1930s—and the need for releases to provide a current to push the fish more quickly down the Snake and the middle Columbia. What they disagree on is the mortality of smolts at the dams under various spill and transportation options undertaken under shifting river conditions.

The quarrel essentially is about what to do when the fish reach the dams: should they be spilled over the top or barged? On the virtual river scientists battle over modifications of two strategies that have already failed in unmodified forms on the actual river: barging and spills. CRiSP suggests that with an improved collection system, barging, particularly in low-water years, is the preferred solution and has worked better than is realized. FLUSH suggests spills.

There are no startling new options, and CRiSP modelers think that there are no dramatic and easy answers. Removing the dams might restore the salmon, but despite some environmentalist bravado, this almost certainly will not happen. And on the virtual river all the easier steps fail, by themselves, to yield dramatic results.

And what won't work on the virtual river is unlikely to work on the actual Columbia, for the virtual river is a much nicer and less complicated place. That is the appeal of virtuality. On the Columbia powerful interests have become dependent on the organic machine, and they feel pressed into a corner by mounting demands on the river.

Salmon inspire fear along the river. The BPA needs the river's dams for its existence, and the BPA, burdened by debt and embarrassing failures, faces its own projections of insufficient power supply. The thirty-year purchase of Canada's share of power (the Canadian Entitlement) produced by the Columbia River Treaty begins to expire before the end of the century. In the fall of 1994 American and Canadian negotiators have tentatively agreed to pay British Columbia $5 billion for its downstream power rights on the Columbia. Power managers, already running deficits, fear allocating this expensive water, supposed to produce electricity, to flushing salmon downstream. When they put lost revenue against wild salmon, they see million-dollar fish. The aluminum industry, pushed by foreign competition, already closing plants, fears increasing costs. Farmers, buffeted by constant crisis and fearful of losing their own subsidies, see the salmon forcing modification in the rivers that will increase their costs. Barge operators fear changes in the river that could drive them from business entirely. Environmentalists, faced with the end of even more wild runs, fear for the salmon. They see the current battle as a last stand for Columbia River wild salmon. And the Columbia River Indians, having validated their rights to catch a fish that has been at the center of their common life for millennia, find the fish gone. They have demonstrated their new power and standing by helping to force the issue on the decline of the salmon. They have the legal standing to demand that the Columbia's salmon be saved. They are left to savor the bitterness of a promise broken even in its keeping. Saving the salmon means, at least for now, barring most fishing on the river. Half of nothing is nothing.

III

The Columbia has become an organic machine which human beings manage without fully understanding what they have created. The organic machine has, in turn, spawned a virtual river whose life influences the actual Columbia. Mumford and Emerson foresaw part of this. They grasped how the human and the natural, the mechanical and the organic, had merged so that the two could never be ultimately distinguished. We live with the consequences.

Ring up the costs of the last half century of development along the Columbia and they are immense. Development has largely destroyed a vast natural bounty of salmon and replaced it with an expensive and declining artificial system of hatcheries. In producing plutonium, Hanford took innocent lives and still threatens the pollution of the land and the river long after present generations are gone. The Bureau of Reclamation did create new farmlands, but these farmlands brought with

them an exploitive set of labor relations and produced expensive subsidized crops that were ultimately not needed. The great problem of
American agriculture after World War II was surplus, not shortage.
The BPA created a vast power system, but one that never achieved its
own social ends. The river delivered much of its power to a few large
industrial plants that employed relatively few people. The BPA finally
overextended itself with the WPPSS debacle that resulted in the loss of
billions of dollars badly needed elsewhere. I have purposely made the
list one-sided to mirror and counter the self-congratulatory propaganda
that still stems from the various "miracles" that arose at the Grand
Coulee, at Hanford, and in the Columbia Basin.

Such failures have produced some astonishing debits over the last
twenty years. There are the billions of dollars lost on WPPSS; there are
the hidden subsidies to the Columbia Basin Project. There is the more
than $1 billion spent trying to repair the damage done to salmon. There
is the roughly $5 billion to be paid to British Columbia over the next
thirty years for its share of Columbia electricity. There is $3 billion
spent to clean up Hanford, with far more to come. Many of these
contribute to, but don't completely account for, the BPA budget deficits
of recent years. A lot of money flows down this river.

And yet simply to renounce development on the Columbia is equally
to miss the point. We can't treat the river as if it is simply nature and
all dams, hatcheries, channels, pumps, cities, ranches, and pulp mills
are ugly and unnecessary blotches on a still coherent natural system.
These things are now part of the river itself. There are reasons they are
there. They are not going to vanish, and they cannot simply be erased.
Some would reduce the consequences to a cautionary tale of the need
to leave nature alone. But to do so is to lose the central insight of the
Columbia: there is no clear line between us and nature. The Columbia,
an organic machine, a virtual river, is at once our creation and retains
a life of its own beyond our control.

At the end of his life, Lewis Mumford, whose earlier work so clearly
reflected the social currents that reshaped the mid-twentieth-century
Columbia, wrote a final major book: *The Pentagon of Power*. In some
ways it reflected Mumford at his worst: it was dire, portentous, totalizing,
and omniscient. It cut against much of the social analysis that informs
this volume. I see contest, conflict, division, and compromise where
Mumford saw a relentless and triumphant megamachine. But I am

unwilling to dismiss *The Pentagon of Power*. A moral urgency propelled Mumford: a recognition that something had gone terribly wrong in modern society, that its roots must be discovered and the problem fixed. Mumford saw the problem as one of power, that protean word that can mean energy, the ability to labor and effect change, as well as the capacity to command both energy and labor. He saw human beings in conflict with nature. He located the site of conflict at the point where the mechanical and the organic meet, at the point where humans confront complex systems and seek to alter them to produce relatively simple ends, at the point where science seeks to effect all things possible, and where social groups struggle to control the results. That site in this book is the Columbia River.

In the end, one of the intellectual architects of the organic machine inveighed against runaway mechanistic thinking. And certainly on the Columbia mechanistic thinking has both dominated the river and failed to control what it has produced. Machines can be disassembled. They can move from place to place. They can be put to varying uses. In turning the Columbia into a machine, we have done all of these things.

In treating the Columbia as a machine we have literally and conceptually disassembled the river. It has become to its users a set of separate spaces and parts. Fishermen see habitat. Irrigators see water. Power managers, utility operators, and those who run aluminum factories see reservoirs necessary to turn turbines. Barge owners see channels with certain depths of water. Environmentalists see brief stretches of free-flowing water. All stake a social claim to their part of the machine. None of them are concerned with the river as a whole.

This is not simply a commodification of the river; our treatment of the Columbia has moved well beyond that. The river is not just water flowing through its original bed that has been divided up and apportioned among many users. Because the river has become an organic machine, a partial human creation, each of the groups claiming the river has created part of what they claim. They dramatically rearrange the physical space of the river. Salmon, for example, once used virtually the whole river; they demanded most of its space. But the attempts to produce salmon in hatcheries reallocate space. Salmon naturally "ripen" as they swim upriver to spawn; hatcheries divert salmon from their home streams and their journeys; they replace the space of the river and the stream with the holding pond. Salmon whose ancestors spawned on gravel beds now yield their eggs to the knife and the eggs are fertilized and matured in tanks. This was not just claiming the river; this was a dramatic reallocation of space, a truncating of the river that the salmon once knew.

The same reallocation and social creation of space takes place all along the Columbia. Irrigation farmers not only take water from the Columbia, they commandeer waterways nature had once used and have built other artificial streams to contain water pumped from the river. This network of ditches and canals, however, never stands totally alone. Artificial channels merge with existing hydrologic patterns and movements. Similarly, the dams on the Columbia do not simply depend on the run of the river to turn the turbines. The creation of huge reservoirs allows some control over the flow of the river itself. These reservoirs, too, reapportion space. They bury what had once been land. They turn flowing water into still water. Shallow water becomes deep water. The examples could go on and on. People with quite specific social and economic interests are not just fighting over ownership of a piece of nature. They are fighting over something they in part create but which contains within it, at its heart, something they have not made. This unmade world is what we call nature.

There is a tourist performance every summer at the Grand Coulee Dam. At night the dam becomes a screen for a massive light show. The pretense of the show is that the Columbia River narrates its own history. Humans give the Columbia a voice and speak for it. One of the images projected on the dam is a representation of the land and river buried by Lake Roosevelt, the dam's reservoir. The Columbia suddenly appears in the night as it supposedly was before the dam. It is the ghost of nature within the machine, but, of course, the representation is merely light that the machine itself produces: it is not nature, it is an artifact of human technology. But, in another sense, it is nature. The light on the dam is just as much a product of the vast natural cycles of the planet, now channeled into a piece of technology created by human labor, as the original river was. There is no easy way to disentangle the natural and cultural here.

What is real is the mixture, and we seem unable to come to terms with this even though we have created it. Mumford's jeremiad against the megamachine recognizes that we treat nature as if it were literally a machine that can be disassembled and redesigned largely at will, as if its various parts can be assigned different functions with only a technical relation to other parts and functions. But the Columbia is not just a machine. It is an *organic* machine. Our tendency to break it into parts does not work. For no matter how much we have created many of its spaces and altered its behavior, it is still tied to larger organic cycles beyond our control.

Dams, hatcheries, channels, pumps, cities, and ranches are all products of human work, and it is our labor that ultimately links us to the river. Our labor, our energy, is the nature in us. And we harness it, just as we harness nature, to social purposes. It is the purposes that matter. And all the purposes that went into the harnessing of the river were not bad. The visions of Indian peoples have power still. Their labor holds them to the river yet. The gillnetters' vision of a life of labor rewarded by nature remains in many ways a noble one. The dreams that progressive planners had for the dams imagined not just production but justice. They still have the power to stir. The hopes given voice in Woody Guthrie's lyrics move us yet. Even Hanford was propelled by the belief that what was at stake was nothing less than the fate of human freedom. Humans live in the world; they bring their passions as well as their interests to it. How we use nature, how we have used and will use the Columbia, are about ways of life, about work, justice, and dreams for our children. There is no retreating from that even if we wished to.

The past, like it or not, is always with us. Americans are impatient with history. But human actions on the Columbia have produced a long history, and history has consequences. Human history and the history of the river have merged to create the modern Columbia, which is at once a natural space and a social space. It is an organic machine and has to be dealt with as such. To call for a return to nature is posturing. It is a religious ritual in which the recantation of our sins and a pledge to sin no more promises to restore purity. Some people believe sins go away. History does not go away.

Our society faces exactly the kind of dilemma it is least prepared to deal with; the quarrels on the Columbia cannot be settled by dividing the pie. Dividing the Columbia up among users has not worked and will not work. Nor can a solution be found by reducing uses to dollars and selecting the most valuable ones. The river has purposes of its own which do not readily yield to desires to maximize profit, and in any case, battles over the Columbia have not been purely economic. The logic of economists has fashioned one debacle after another. Arguments over the river proceed as if everyone speaks about one river in one tongue. But, in fact, this is a river subdivided into separate spaces whose users speak to each other in a babel of discourses: law, religion, nature talk, economics, science, and more. The experts and regulators empowered to solve the river's problems only bare our divisions.

As the century comes to an end, the river we have partially created changes before our eyes, mocking our supposed control. It changes, and as it changes, it makes clear the insufficiencies of our own science, society, and notions of justice and value. The Columbia runs through the heart of the Northwest in ways we have never imagined. It flows along the borders of the numerous divisions in our fractured society. To come to terms with the Columbia, we need to come to terms with it as a whole, as an organic machine, not only as a reflection of our own social divisions but as the site in which these divisions play out. If the conversation is not about fish and justice, about electricity and ways of life, about production and nature, about beauty as well as efficiency, and about how these things are inseparable in our own tangled lives, then we have not come to terms with our history on this river.

BIBLIOGRAPHICAL ESSAY

Much of this book is the result of archival research. The Oregon Historical Society is a critical source for the early Columbia. I used John C. Ainsworth, Reminiscences, Mss 504-1; Columbia River Improvement Association, Scrapbook, 1903, Mss 2907-1; Edward Beard, Diaries and Reminiscence, Mss 1509. The Columbia River Fishermen's Protective Union, Letterbook, Astoria, Oregon, microfilm copy. The Historical Society also has useful collections for the twentieth century, particularly the Delbert Norton Papers and Ralph Cowgill Papers.

Collections at the Manuscripts and Archives Division, University of Washington Library, complemented the OHC collections, but they are more useful for the twentieth century. I found the Walter Barnes Papers, Willis Batcheller Papers, Carl Magnusson Papers, Harlan Holmes Papers, S. F. Hutton Papers, George Yantis Papers, Warren G. Magnuson Papers, Columbia Basin Inter-Agency Committee Papers, Nancy Thomas Papers, Herbert Parker Papers, and Henry M. Jackson Papers particularly useful.

The most critical sources for the mid-twentieth-century Columbia come from the National Archives. The records of the National Resources Planning Board, Record Group 187, Correspondence and Related Records, 1933–1943, National Archives, Pacific NW Region, are essential. Less useful are the records of the U.S. Army Corps of Engineers, Portland District, Record Group 77, Civil Works Project Files, 1910–1983. The records of the Bureau of Indian Affairs, RG 75, NA, PNW Region, contain essential information on later fishing rights struggles.

For a general background on the geomorphology of streams and energy dynamics, I relied on Luna B. Leopold, *Water: A Primer* (San Francisco: W. H. Freeman, 1974); R. R. Curry, "Rivers: A Geomorphic and Chemical

Overview," in Ray T. Oglesby, Clarence A. Carlson, and James A. McCann (eds.), *River Ecology and Man* (New York: Academic Press, 1972); and Marie Morisawa, *Streams: Their Dynamics and Morphology* (New York: McGraw-Hill, 1968).

For the concept of energy, see Daniel M. Siegel, "The Energy Concept: A Historical Overview," *Materials and Society*, vol. 7 (1983), and for discussions of energy, power, work, and human society, see Timothy J. Healy, *Energy and Society* (San Francisco: Boyd & Fraser, 1976), and D. S. L. Cardwell, *Technology, Science & History* (London: Heinemann, 1972).

In looking at the early relations of human labor and nature on the Columbia, I relied on Alexander Ross, *Adventures of the First Settlers on the Oregon or Columbia River*, Milo M. Quaife (ed.) (New York: Citadel Press, 1969; original edition, 1849); Alexander Ross, *The Fur Hunters of the Far West* (Norman: University of Oklahoma Press, 1956); Gabriel Franchère, *Journal of a Voyage on the North West Coast of North America During the Years 1811, 1812, 1813 and 1814* (Toronto: Champlain Society, 1969); Gary Moulton (ed.), *The Journals of the Lewis and Clark Expedition* (Lincoln: University of Nebraska Press, 1983–); Philip Ashton Rollins (ed.), *The Discovery of the Oregon Trail: Robert Stuart's Narratives of His Overland Trip Eastward from Astoria in 1812–1813* (New York: Charles Scribner's Sons, 1935); Frederick Merk, *Fur Trade and Empire: George Simpson's Journal* (Cambridge: Harvard University Press, 1931); David Douglas, *Journal Kept by David Douglas During His Travels in North America, 1823–1827 . . .* (London: William Wesley & Son, 1914); Samuel Parker, *Journal of an Exploring Tour Beyond the Rocky Mountains . . .* (Ithaca, N.Y.: Published by the Author, 1838); A. J. Allen (compiler), *Ten Years in Oregon: Travels and Adventures of Doctor E. White and Lady, West of the Rocky Mountains . . .* (Ithaca, N.Y.: Press of Andrus, Gauntlett, & Co., 1850); Burt B. Barker, *Letters of Dr. John McLoughlin Written at Fort Vancouver, 1829–1832* (Portland: Binfords & Mort, 1948); P. J. De Smet, *Letters and Sketches: With a Narrative of a Year's Residence Among the Indian Tribes of the Rocky Mountains*, in Reuben G. Thwaites (ed.), *Early Western Travels* (Cleveland: Arthur H. Clark, 1906), vol. 27; Joel Palmer, *Journal of Travels over the Rocky Mountains to the Mouth of the Columbia River: Made During the Years 1845 and 1846 . . .* in Thwaites, *Early Western Travels*, vol. 30.

For the Indians of the Columbia, I relied heavily on Eugene Hunn, *Nch'i-Wana: "The Big River": Mid-Columbia Indians and Their Land* (Seattle: University of Washington Press, 1988), and Yvonne P. Hajda, "Regional Social Organization in the Greater Lower Columbia 1792–1830" (Ph.D. Dissertation, University of Washington, 1984). But I also used Leslie Spier and Edward Sapir, *Wishram Ethnography*, University of Washington Publications in Anthropology, vol. 3, no. 3, May 1930 (Seattle: University of Washington Press, 1930), pp. 174–76; David French, "Wasco-Wishram," in Edward H. Spicer (ed.), *Perspectives in American Indian Culture Change* (Chicago: University of

Chicago Press, 1961); Randall F. Schalk, "The Structure of an Anadromous Fish Resource," in Lewis R. Binford (ed.), *For Theory Building in Archaeology: Essays on Faunal Remains, Aquatic Resources, Spatial Analysis, and Systemic Modeling* (New York: Academic Press, 1977); Verne F. Ray, "The Sanpoil and Nespelem: Salishan Peoples of Northeastern Washington" (M.A. Thesis, University of Washington, 1933); Gordon Winant Hewes, "Aboriginal Use of Fishery Resources in Northwestern North America" (Ph.D. Dissertation, University of California at Berkeley, 1947); Harry Holbert Turner-High, *Ethnography of the Kutenai*, Memoirs of the American Anthropological Association, no. 56 (Menasha, Wisc.: AAA, 1941); Robert T. Boyd, "The Introduction of Diseases Among the Indians of the Pacific Northwest, 1774–1874" (Ph.D. Dissertation, University of Washington, 1985).

Joseph Taylor's master's thesis, "Steelhead's Mother Was His Father Salmon: Development and Declension of Aboriginal Conservation in the Oregon Country Salmon Fishery" (M.A. Thesis, University of Oregon, 1992), is very useful for understanding the early Oregon Indian fishers. Donald Parman, "Inconstant Advocacy: The Erosion of Indian Fishing Rights in the Pacific Northwest, 1933–1956," *Pacific Historical Review*, vol. 53 (May 1984), is the best account of later controversies. See also *Indian Fishing Rights*, Hearings Before the Subcommittee on Indian Affairs of the Committee on Interior and Insular Affairs, U.S. Senate, 88th Cong., 2nd Sess., on S.J. Res. 170 and S.J. Res. 171 . . . , August 5 and 6, 1964 (Washington, D.C.: Government Printing Office, 1964).

For Northwest Indian texts, see Melville Jacobs, *Northwest Sahaptin Texts*, University of Washington Publications in Anthropology, vol. 2, no. 6 (Seattle: University of Washington Press, 1925); Franz Boas (ed.), *Folk-Tales of Salishan and Sahaptin Tribes* (New York: Draus Reprint, 1969; original edition, Lancaster, Pa., and New York: American Folk-Lore Society, 1917); Franz Boas, *Chinook Texts*, Bulletin 20, Bureau of Ethnology, Smithsonian Institution (Washington, D.C.: Government Printing Office, 1894); Melville Jacobs, *Kalapuya Texts*, Part I, Santiam Kalapuya Ethnologic Texts (Seattle: University of Washington Press, 1945); Albert S. Gatschet, Leo J. Rachtenberg, and Melville Jacobs, *Kalapuya Texts*, Part III (Seattle: University of Washington Press, 1935); Edward Sapir (ed.), *Wishram Texts*, Publications of the American Ethnological Society, vol. 2 (Leyden: E. J. Brill, 1909).

The best introduction to Columbia River salmon fishing is Courtland Smith, *Salmon Fishers of the Columbia* (Corvallis: Oregon State University Press, 1979). Despite its anti-Indian bias, Anthony Netboy, *The Columbia River Salmon and Steelhead Trout: Their Fight for Survival* (Seattle: University of Washington Press, 1980), is useful, as is a federal study, Joseph A. Craig and Robert L. Hacker, "The History and Development of the Fisheries of the Columbia River," *Bulletin of the Bureau of Fisheries*, vol. 49 (1940). I found the work of Peter Larkin very helpful: "Pacific Salmon: Scenarios for the Future," Donald L. McKernan Lectures in Marine Affairs, University of Washington, April 15–17, 1980 (Seattle: Institute for Marine Studies, University of Washington, 1980); P. A. Larkin (ed.), *The Investigation of Fish-Power Problems*, H. R. MacMillan Lectures in Fisheries, Symposium Held at the University of British Columbia, April 29 and 30, 1957 (Vancouver, B.C.: Institute of Fisheries, University of British Columbia, 1958). For fish wheels, see Ivan J. Donaldson and Frederick K. Cramer, *Fishwheels of the Columbia* (Portland, Ore.: Binfords & Mort, 1971). For examples of early attempts to protect salmon: *Save the Columbia River Salmon: Brief Submitted to the Federal Power Commission in Opposition to Application of Washington Irrigation and Development Company for a License to Construct a Dam Across the Columbia River at Priest Rapids, Washington* (Olympia: Frank M. Bamborn, 1924).

The technical literature on the salmon fisheries is overwhelming. I give only a small sample here. The place to start is William G. Pearcy, *Ocean Ecology of North Pacific Salmonids* (Seattle: University of Washington Press, 1992). A series of specialized studies by Leonard A. Fulton also proved a useful guide to orienting a nonspecialist as to salmon habitats: Leonard Fulton, "Spawning Areas and Abundance of Chinook Salmon (*Oncorhynchus tshawytscha*) in the Columbia River Basin—Past and Present," *Special Scientific Report—Fisheries No. 571*, U.S. Department of the Interior, Fish and Wildlife Service, Bureau of Commercial Fisheries (Washington, D.C., October 1968); Leonard A. Fulton, "Spawning Areas and Abundance of Steelhead Trout and Coho, Sockeye, and Chum Salmon in the Columbia River Basin—Past and Present," *Special Scientific Report—Fisheries No. 618*, U.S. Department of Commerce, National Oceanic and Atmospheric Administration, National Marine Fisheries Service (Washington, D.C., 1970).

For a sample of the nineteenth-century literature, see Report of Chas. F. Powell, February 23, 1887, Letter from the Secretary of War, Transmitting, in Response to Senate Resolution of January 27, 1887, Report on the Salmon Fisheries of the Columbia River, Senate Executive Document 123, 50th Cong., 1st Sess. The annual *Report of the Commissioner of Fish and Fisheries* is helpful. Also see Barton W. Evermann, "A Preliminary Report upon Salmon Investigations in Idaho in 1894," *Bulletin of the United States Fish Commission*, vol. 15 for 1895 (Washington, D.C.: Government Printing Office, 1896). Major W. A. Jones, "The Salmon Fisheries of the Columbia River," Senate Executive Document 123, 50th Cong., 1st Sess.

For the twentieth-century fishery, the sources are so numerous that I will list only the ones I repeatedly cited or quoted in this book. Willis H. Rich, "Early History and Seaward Migration of Chinook Salmon in the Columbia and Sacramento Rivers," *Bulletin of the Bureau of Fisheries*, vol. 37, 1919–20, Document no. 887 (Washington, D.C.: Government Printing Office, 1920); R. E. Foerster, "A Comparison of the Natural and Artificial Propagation of Salmon," *Transactions of the American Fisheries Society*, 61st Annual Meeting,

September 21, 22, 23, 1931; Special Symposium Issue, *Stanford Ichthyological Bulletin*, vol. 1 (May 3, 1940), particularly Willis H. Rich, "Fishery Problems Raised by the Development of Water Resources," Harlan B. Holmes, "The Passage of Fish at Bonneville Dam," and Wilbert Mcleod Chapman, "Fish Problems Connected with the Grand Coulee Dam"; *A Program of Rehabilitation of the Columbia River Fisheries, Prepared Jointly by State of Washington Department of Fisheries, State of Oregon, Oregon Fish Commission, in Cooperation with U.S. Fish and Wildlife Service* (n.p., 1947); Frederic F. Fish and Mitchell G. Hanavan, "A Report upon the Grand Coulee Fish-Maintenance Project, 1939–1947," *Special Scientific Report No. 55*, Fish and Wildlife Service, U.S. Department of the Interior (Washington, D.C., 1948); Informal Committee on Chinook and Coho, *Reports by the United States and Canada on the Status, Ocean Migrations and Exploitation of Northeast Pacific Stocks of Chinook and Coho Salmon, to 1964*, vol. 2: Report by the Canadian Section (1969); Q. J. Stober et al., "Columbia River Irrigation Withdrawal Environmental Review: Columbia River Fishery Study," Final Report, June 15–October 15, 1979, Contract with Department of the Army, Portland District Corps of Engineers, FRI-UW-7919; "Summary Report: Nitrogen Supersaturation in the Columbia and Snake Rivers," July 1971, Environmental Protection Agency, Region X (Seattle, 1971).

Among trade journals, the *Pacific Fisherman* is useful for early in the century. See, for example, Harlan Holmes, "The Problem at Bonneville," *Pacific Fisherman*, June 1934; "Cut in Fishway Appropriation Endangers Columbia River Salmon," *Pacific Fisherman*, March 1935; "The Fishways at Bonneville," *Pacific Fisherman*, September 1935. Currently Bill Rudolph's coverage of the Columbia River and salmon for the *Alaska Fisherman's Journal* has been the best available. See, for example, Bill Rudolph, "Fish & Chips," *Alaska Fisherman's Journal*, June 1993; "Downmouth," *Alaska Fisherman's Journal*, March 1993; "Near Death Experience," *Alaska Fisherman's Journal*, December 1993; "Up a Lazy River," *Alaska Fisherman's Journal*, April 1993.

State reports are also useful for both fisheries and power. See, for example, Fourteenth Oregon Legislative Assembly, 1887, *Report of the Special Committee to Examine into and Investigate the Fishing Industry of this State* (Salem: Frank C. Baker, 1893); "Report of the Preliminary Investigations into the Possible Methods of Preserving the Columbia River Salmon and Steelhead at the Grand Coulee Dam . . . ," Report Prepared for the U.S. Bureau of Reclamation, Department of Fisheries, State of Washington (January 1938); Frank Haw et al., "Development of Washington State Salmon Sport Fishery Through 1964," *Research Bulletin No. 7* (State of Washington, Department of Fisheries, May 1967); James B. Haas, "Fishery Problems Associated with Brownlee, Oxbow, and Hells Canyon Dams on the Middle Snake River," *Investigational Report No. 4* (Fish Commission of Oregon, Portland, January 1965). These represent but a small sample of an extensive list of fishery publications that are too numerous to cite here.

For labor and the canning process, Chris Friday's *Organizing Asian American Labor: The Pacific Coast Canned Salmon Industry: 1870–1942* (Philadelphia: Temple University Press) is indispensable. Also see Gordon Dodds, *The Salmon King of Oregon: R. D. Hume and the Pacific Fisheries* (Chapel Hill: University of North Carolina Press, 1963). *Columbia River Fishermen's Protective Union . . .* (Astoria, Ore.: G. W. Snyder, 1890).

For the development of agriculture and transportation, see Henry Villard, *Memoirs of Henry Villard, Journalist and Financier, 1835–1900* (Boston: Houghton Mifflin, 1904); James B. Hedges, *Henry Villard and the Railways of the Northwest* (New Haven: Yale University Press, 1930); Donald W. Meinig, *The Great Columbia Plain* (Seattle: University of Washington Press, 1968).

In framing my arguments on work and leisure, I found an annotated edition of Rudyard Kipling, "American Salmon: A Sketch from American Notes," *Pacific Northwest Quarterly*, vol. 60 (October 1969), very useful, and, of course, I relied heavily on Ralph Waldo Emerson, *Essays and Lectures* (New York: Library of America, 1983). His essays "Nature," "The Poet," and "The Young American" were particularly important. In examining the relations of nature and technology, I was reminded of how important a book Leo Marx's *The Machine in the Garden: Technology and the Pastoral Ideal in America* (New York: Oxford University Press, 1964) really is.

For early modifications of the Columbia, William F. Willingham, "Engineering the Cascades Canal and Locks, 1876–1896," *Oregon Historical Quarterly*, vol. 88 (Fall 1987). To follow later modifications, however, it is necessary to use manuscript sources cited above.

For a background to waterpower, electricity, and dams, see Louis C. Hunter, *A History of Industrial Power in the United States*, vol. 1: *Water Power in the Century of the Steam Engine* (Charlottesville: University of Virginia Press, 1979), and Thomas Hughes, *Networks of Power: Electrification in Western Society, 1880–1930* (Baltimore: Johns Hopkins University Press, 1988).

For good accounts of New Deal development and the environment on the Columbia, see Richard Lowitt, *The New Deal in the West* (Bloomington: Indiana University Press, 1984), and David Coe, "Realms of Nature, Spheres of Interest: Environmental Policy in the Pacific Northwest" (Ph.D. Dissertation, Stanford University, 1993). Charles McKinley, *Uncle Sam in the Pacific Northwest: Federal Management of Natural Resources in the Columbia River Valley* (Berkeley: University of California Press, 1952), remains an important source for this period. For public power in the Pacific Northwest, the starting point is Wesley Arden Dick, "Visions of Abundance: The Public Power Crusade in the Pacific Northwest in the Era of J. D. Ross and the New Deal" (Ph.D. Dissertation, University of Washington, 1973). For private utilities, see Craig Wollner, *Electrifying Eden: Portland General Electric, 1889–1965* (Portland:

Oregon Historical Society Press, 1990). Much of the long struggle for development on the Columbia is contained in federal and state reports and documents. See Federal Power Commission, *Report to the Federal Power Commission on the Uses of the Upper Columbia River* (Washington, D.C.: Government Printing Office, 1923); *The Columbia Basin Project*, Hearings Before the Committee on Irrigation and Reclamation, House of Representatives, 70th Cong., 1st Sess., on H.R. 7029, January 16–17, 1928 (Washington, D.C.: Government Printing Office, 1928); and the so-called 308 Report, because it was a response to H.R. Document 308, *The Columbia River and Minor Tributaries*, 73rd Cong., 1st Sess., House Document 103 (Washington, D.C.: Government Printing Office, 1933). John H. Lewis, "The Columbia River Power Project Near the Dalles, Oregon," Office of the State Engineer, Bulletin No. 3 (Salem, Ore., January 1912). An Address by Herbert Hoover . . . Before the Columbia River Basin League, Seattle, August 21, 1926. *Columbia River and Its Tributaries*, Hearings Before the Subcommittee of the Committee on Irrigation and Reclamation, House of Representatives, 78th Cong., 1st Sess., under H.R. 262, part 4, Hearings at Lewiston, Idaho, August 31, 1943, Hearings at Portland, Ore., September 10, 1943 (Washington, D.C.: Government Printing Office, 1944); U.S. Department of the Interior, *The Columbia River: A Comprehensive Report on the Development of the Water Resources of the Columbia River Basin for Irrigation, Power Production, and Other Beneficial Uses in Idaho, Montana, Nevada, Oregon, Utah, Washington, and Wyoming*, Sponsored by and Prepared Under the General Supervision of the Bureau of Reclamation, February 1947 (Washington, D.C.: Government Printing Office, 1947). Hearings on the later dams are very useful, for example: *On the Improvement of the Columbia River (Foster Creek Dam)*, Wash., Hearings Before the Committee on Rivers and Harbors, House of Representatives, 79th Cong., 2nd Sess. (Washington, D.C.: Government Printing Office, 1946); Hearings Before a Subcommittee of the Committee on the Merchant Marine and Fisheries, House of Representatives, 79th Cong., 2nd Sess., Pursuant to the Authority of H.R. 38 . . . July 1, 1946 (Washington D.C.: Government Printing Office, 1946).

For popular writings on hydropower and fish in the 1920s, 1930s, and 1940s and discussions of superpower and Giant Power, see Chester G. Gilbert and Joseph E. Pogue, *America's Power Resources: The Economic Significance of Coal, Oil, and Water-Power* (New York: Century, 1921); "The Power Situation in the United States," *Science*, N.S. 48, no. 1240 (October 4, 1918), and series of articles *The Survey*, vol. 51 (March 1, 1924); Richard L. Neuberger, "The Biggest Thing on Earth: Grand Coulee Dam," *Harper's* (February 1937); Katherine Glover, "Planning for Power," *Survey Graphic*, vol. 25 (October 1936); Richard L. Neuberger, "The Columbia Flows to the Land," *Survey Graphic*, vol. 28 (July 1939); Katherine Glover, *America Begins Again* (New York: Whittlesey House, 1939); Stuart Chase, "A Vision in Kilowatts," *Fortune* (April

1933); "Washington State Grange Attitude Toward Columbia Basin Development Explained," *Grange News*, June 20, 1931; Richard L. Neubérger, "The Great Salmon Experiment," *Harper's* (February 1945).

Robert Ficken is coming out with a new biography of Rufus Woods: *Rufus Woods, The Columbia River and the Building of Modern Washington*. See also Bruce Mitchell, "Rufus Woods and Columbia River Development," *Pacific Northwest Quarterly*, vol. 52 (October 1961). A collection of Woods's own papers is available at the *Wenatchee Daily World*, and Woods essentially gives his own account in Rufus Woods, *The 23 Year Battle for Grand Coulee Dam* (Wenatchee, Wash.: Wenatchee Daily World, 1944). For a popular account of the struggle for the dam that is an extended paean to James O'Sullivan, see George Sundborg, *Hail Columbia: The Thirty-Year Struggle for Grand Coulee Dam* (New York: Macmillan, 1954). Also see chapters in Richard L. Neuberger, *Our Promised Land* (Moscow: University of Idaho Press, 1989; original edition, 1938).

For the Columbia Basin Project, see a fine dissertation by Paul C. Pitzer, "Visions, Plans, and Realities: A History of the Columbia Basin Project" (Ph.D. Dissertation, University of Oregon, 1990). For an example of contemporary hopes, R. M. Turner, "The Columbia Basin Irrigation Project," *Extension Service Review*, September 1941; Richard L. Neuberger, "The Columbia Flows to the Land," *Survey Graphic*, vol. 28 (July 1939).

There are abundant popular reports on the Grand Coulee and later dams: *Grand Coulee Dam: The Eighth Wonder of the World* (Davenport, Wash.: Times Publishing Company, 1947); *The Grand Coulee Dam and the Columbia Basin Reclamation Project*, U.S. Department of the Interior, Bureau of Reclamation (n.d.); Bob Woods, *Kilowatts and Salmon: A Look at the Cost and Benefits of Preserving the Spawning Grounds and Habits of Commercial Salmon in the Upper Columbia River*, reprinted from a series appearing in the *Wenatchee Daily World*, February 27 to March 10, 1958.

The critical figure for understanding the hopes of progressive planners was Lewis Mumford. Mumford's key works for regionalism and planning in the 1930s were *Technics and Civilization* (New York: Harcourt, Brace, 1934), *The Culture of Cities* (New York: Harcourt, Brace, 1938), and *Regional Planning in the Pacific Northwest: A Memorandum* (Portland, Ore.: Northwest Regional Council, 1939). For the later Mumford, see *The Myth of the Machine*, vol. 2: *The Pentagon of Power* (New York: Harcourt Brace Jovanovich, 1970). For Mumford's life and thought, see Donald L. Miller, *Lewis Mumford: A Life* (New York: Weidenfeld & Nicolson, 1989), and Casey N. Blake, *Beloved Community: The Cultural Criticism of Randolph Bourne, Van Wyck Brooks, Waldo Frank, & Lewis Mumford* (Chapel Hill: University of North Carolina Press, 1990).

Philip Fuingiello, *Toward a National Power Policy: The New Deal and the Electric Utility Industry, 1933–1941* (Pittsburgh: University of Pittsburgh Press,

1973), and Herman Voeltz, "Genesis and Development of a Regional Power Agency in the Pacific Northwest, 1933–43," *Pacific Northwest Quarterly*, vol. 53 (1962), are two of several studies that cover the beginning of the Bonneville Power Administration. There is, however, no good academic study of the BPA, although there are two useful official histories: Gus Norwood, *Power for the People: A History of Policies of the Bonneville Power Administration*, and Gene Tollefson, *BPA & the Struggle for Power at Cost* (Portland, Ore.: Bonneville Power Administration, n.d.). The BPA library in Portland, which is not exactly welcoming to outside researchers, does have a good collection of printed materials, technical reports, etc. The annual reports of the Bonneville Power Administration are also useful.

For the present-day BPA and the Columbia, see the agency's annual reports, various environmental impact statements such as *Final Environmental Statement: Wholesale Power Rate Increase* (Washington, D.C.: U.S. Department of the Interior, Bonneville Power Administration, 1974). Kai N. Lee and Donna Lee Klemka, with Marion E. Marts, *Electric Power and the Future of the Pacific Northwest* (Seattle: University of Washington Press, 1980), is very useful to understanding Bonneville and WPPSS. A good introduction to WPPSS is Daniel Jack Chasan, *The Fall of the House of WPPSS* (Seattle: Sasquatch Books, 1985).

For Canada and the United States, see *Analysis and Progress Report: Cooperative Development of the Columbia River Basin Water Resources, Canada and the United States* (October 1960); "Discussion of Coordinated Operation of Electric Utility Systems in the Pacific Northwest in Conjunction with Canadian Storage, Presentation Before the Treaty Negotiating Team, Washington, D.C., January 13, 1961," Special Collections, University of Washington Library; John V. Krutilla, *The Columbia River Treaty: The Economics of an International River Basin Development* (Baltimore: Johns Hopkins University Press, 1967); W. R. Derrick Swell, "The Columbia River Treaty and Protocol Agreement," *Natural Resources Journal*, vol. 4 (October 1964); John V. Krutilla, *Sequence and Timing in River Basin Development with Special Application to Canadian–United States Columbia River Basin Planning*, Resources for the Future, February 1960 (Baltimore: Johns Hopkins University Press, 1960); M. E. Marts, "Upstream Storage Problems in Columbia River Power Development," *Annals of the Association of American Geographers*, vol. 43 (1954); M. E. Marts, "A Long Step Forward on the Columbia: The Canadian–United States Agreement," *Water Power*, vol. 13 (February 1961); Henry L. Gray, "Boosting the Columbia," *Public Utilities Fortnightly*, vol. 83 (May 22, 1969). For a Canadian view, H. L. Keenleyside, "The Columbia River Agreement," Address to the Advertising and Sales Bureau of the Vancouver Board of Trade, February 10, 1964, Special Collections, University of Washington Library, N Pam 1361.

For Hanford, see Bonnie Baack Pendergrass, "Public Power, Politics, and

Technology in the Eisenhower and Kennedy Years: The Hanford Dual Purpose Reactor Controversy, 1956–62" (Ph.D. Dissertation, University of Washington, 1974); John M. Findlay and Bruce Hevly, "Nuclear Technologies and Nuclear Communities: A History of Hanford and the Tri-Cities, 1942–1993," unpublished manuscript, Hanford History Project, Center for the Study of the Pacific Northwest, University of Washington; Daniel Grossman, "Hanford and Its Early Radioactive Releases," *Pacific Northwest Quarterly*, vol. 64 (January 1994); Michele S. Gerber, *Legend and Legacy: Fifty Years of Defense Production at the Hanford Site*, Report Prepared for the U.S. Department of Energy, Office of Environmental Restoration and Waste Management, March 1, 1992, WHC-MR-0293, Revision 1 (Richland, Wash.: Westinghouse Hanford Company, 1992); Michele Stenehjem Gerber, *On the Home Front: The Cold War Legacy of the Hanford Nuclear Site* (Lincoln: University of Nebraska Press, 1992); D. S. Lewis, "Operating the Hanford Reactors," *Electrical Engineering*, vol. 76 (November 1957); Tim Connor, *Hot Water: Groundwater Contamination at the Nuclear Reservation* (Spokane: Hanford Education Action League, 1986); Summary Report, Phase I of the Hanford Environmental Dose Reconstruction Project, August 1991, Pacific Northwest Laboratory, Richland, Wash., 99352, PNL-7410 HEDR Rev. 1, UC-707.

As the Hanford documents are declassified, they are made available at the Hanford Reading Room in Richland. I have used copies of these documents made by John Findlay and Bruce Hevly. For an account of the building of Hanford: Nell Lewis MacGregor, "I Was at Hanford," unpublished manuscript, Archives and Special Collections, University of Washington Library. Earl Pomeroy, "Hanford: Back to Ghosts and Goats," *The Sunday Oregonian: The Northwest's Own Magazine*, February 24, 1946.

For current planning on the Columbia, see Northwest Power Planning Council, *Draft 1991 Northwest Conservation and Electric Power Plan*, vol. 1 (Portland: Northwest Power Planning Council, 1991); Northwest Power Planning Council, *1987 Columbia River Basin Fish and Wildlife Program* (Portland: Northwest Power Planning Council, 1987); Bonneville Power Administration, U.S. Army Corps of Engineers, U.S. Department of the Interior, Bureau of Reclamation, *Columbia River System Operation Review: Draft Environmental Impact Statement*, July 1994. *Streamline: Columbia River System Operation Review Newsletter* is useful for following the rapid changes in the current Columbia.

INDEX

CHECKING THE DEPTH

Moldings vary in depth, so you will need to make sure when you choose the frame that the rabbet is able to accommodate your picture, matt, plus the hardboard, plus the glass (if any).

Needlepoint and oil paintings can cause particular difficulties if the molding is not deep enough and you may need to increase the depth of the rabbet of the frame with additional wood. It is not necessary to use glass with oil paintings nor with some kinds of needlepoint.

There are many attractive frames to choose from. Pastel colors and light, plain woods are very popular and in keeping with today's lighter decor. Bold primary colors as well as black, silver, traditional gold, and darker plain wood are also available; increasingly chosen for their simplicity are natural wood moldings including pine, hickory, and redwood along with plain woods suitable for decoration, which will be discussed later. These can also look stunning if simply limed and polished.

BELOW: A selection of attractive wood and metal moldings.

COMPLEMENTING THE PICTURE

Embossed designs, both plain wood and gilded, are ideal for complementing traditional landscapes, but try not to combine too elaborate a frame with a fussy or busy picture.

Where possible, choose a shade from the picture which can be highlighted by the frame. What is known as a gold slip may be of use to lighten a darker wooden frame. A thin strip of wood, usually in gold but available in other shades too, called a slip, sits inside the main frame. Slip is sold in lengths which can be mitered just like normal molding.

On occasion you may find it useful to buy a ready-made "swept" frame. These are the traditional-style prefabricated gilt frames (also available in plain or stained wood, oak, mahogany, and so on) which are made to standard sizes and often suit oil paintings and mirrors. They are available in both rectangular and oval shapes.

BUYING MOLDING

You should make allowances, when buying molding, for the amount you will lose when cutting a miter and for making a test cut or two; as mentioned earlier, the ends of the molding may have to be trimmed back before you can use it. Ideally, buy it to the nearest foot, or add a foot or so to the final figure.

To work out the final length needed, first measure the length and width of the artwork or the outside of the matt, if you are using one. Add $1/8$in to each measurement just to ensure the artwork and matt will not be too tight in the frame. Then add the length of each piece, including the allowance, which will give you the measurement of the frame. Then find the width of the molding, multiply it by eight (for eight miters) and add this figure to the figure for the perimeter of the framed item. Then add on the cutting allowance.

When you choose the molding, ensure the lengths you buy match as closely as possible; colors can vary, as can the width. Also check that the molding is not bent, damaged, or warped in any way.

ABOVE: Examples of "swept" frames.

HOW TO CUT MOLDINGS

1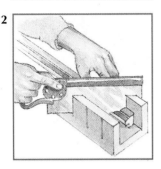

W hen faced with a 10ft length of molding (although smaller lengths are available) it is tempting to ask your supplier to cut it up. If possible, avoid doing this; you will inevitably end up with pieces of molding you cannot use or which are not quite long enough for what you want.

1 If you are using a miter-box, hold the wood firmly (it may be helpful to wedge a bit of cardboard under the rabbet to make it firm).

2 With the rabbet against the far inside of the miter box and with the face of the frame upward, cut the first miter. You should cut about $3/8$in from the end of the molding to make sure you cut the complete angle and to avoid the rough ends of the molding.

2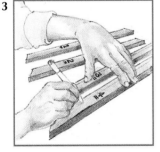

3 Mark each length on the back in pencil as you cut it, 1 and 2 (the long sides), then 3 and 4 (the short sides). Do not try and mark it all at once – work on each length one at a time.

Some woods are softer than others so make sure you saw firmly but without forcing, which may crush the wood. Measure the length of the first leg (cut the long sides first – you can always cut them down if you make a mistake).

3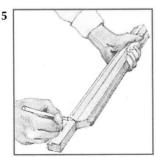

4 Mark the length in pencil on the molding, measuring along the outside edge, and cut to the pencil line, using the appropriate angle and ensuring the back of the molding is at the far edge of the miter-box.

5 Once you have cut length 1, you can use this to show exactly where the second miter should end on length 2. Put the two lengths together so they make a shape like the bow of a ship and mark the miter on 2. Cut it in just the same way as the first.

5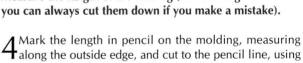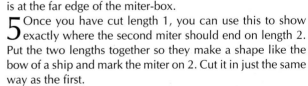

6 Repeat the process for 3 and 4 – the two short sides.

OPPOSITE: Samples of mitered moldings.

Do not sand the rough ends of the miters. If you do this, they may not fit together correctly. The edges can be smoothed very gently with fine glass-paper wrapped around a sanding block, or remove the rough bits with a craft- or trimming-knife. Keep checking that you are not altering the shape, by putting the two ends together and ensuring they make a neat, clean line – you should hardly see the join (hopefully!) when the frame is finished.

The extensive range of matts (also known as mounts) will enable you to select a color, the core (revealed when the bevel is cut) and even the texture of board to suit your picture.

Boards with a black or colored core instead of the normal white/cream core, can provide a readymade border when the bevel is cut – often very effective with black-and-white photographs.

You may also wish to decorate the matt, in which case you will need to think about the color coordination of any rules or borders you wish to add.

You can achieve a similar effect by cutting a double matt, using two boards in complementary colors, one cut to give a narrow border inside the other.

Some boards reflect the stippled effects often used as paint techniques, while others have a textured finish rather than being smooth.

If you are framing a valuable picture, a watercolor, or sketch, it is advisable to choose a conservation or acid-free type of board to prevent any discoloration of the picture as the board ages.

You may also cover a matt in fabric or marbled paper, mitering the corners neatly. Ideally, use a type of adhesive spray which will allow you to move the material or paper around before it is stuck forever!

SIZING THE PICTURE

It is important, before you cut your matt, to decide on the size of the window and what area of the picture you want to show. Many pictures benefit from being "cropped" in this way, drawing you into the focal point more immediately.

A photo of a presentation of a trophy, for example, may look far better with just the two people involved shown, rather than a lot of background. It is also a matter of taste; many posters incorporate wording at the bottom, perhaps giving the name of the artist, gallery, or exhibition. These often use a large amount of white paper below the picture which some people like, but others prefer to take out.

To help you decide on the area, either cut a pair of "masks" – two L-shaped pieces of cardboard – (ensure they are square), approximately 2 inches wide and long enough to accommodate, say, a picture of 16in x 20in or four straight strips of cardboard so you can build up a "frame". Placing them on the picture will allow you to adjust the size of the window, while framing the area you wish to show. Remember that not all pictures have to be rectangular. Accentuating the picture's narrowness or width you can create a far more interesting and attractive result.

OPPOSITE: Sample color matts cut as L-shaped "masks" for sizing the picture with a finished double matt.
NEXT PAGE: A selection of attractive oval-cut matts.

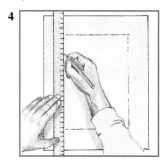

CUTTING THE MATT

Once you have established and noted the size of the window, you must decide on the width of the border. On average, for balance, two or three inches will be sufficient, although some pictures will lend themselves to wider matts. Sometimes, the smallest picture can look effective in a larger matt, while a large poster may not require one at all.

Cutting the window of the matt is not quite as easy as it looks and it is quite difficult to cut a bevel with a trimming- or craft-knife. However, it can be done with practice. The ideal is a matt-cutter designed for the job which has a blade set at an angle of about 60°. The cutter can also be adjusted for boards of different depths and some include a rule with runner grooves to guide you.

Usually, the top and the sides of the matt are of equal width but the bottom is about one-fifth deeper for it to look balanced. For example, the top and the sides could be $2^{3}/_{4}$in and the bottom 3in.

1 Do not presume the matt board is square to start with. Use a set-square to check.

2 Cut the board to the size you need with a trimming-knife (you do not need a bevel for the outside of the matt).

Cut against the vertical edge of a steel rule, not against its bevel edge, and right on the line drawn with the pencil.

3 Decide on the width of each border, then add each measurement to the corresponding dimensions of the window and mark the overall width and height of the matt on the back of the board.

You should always mark and cut the matt board from the back. Erasing pencil lines on the front surface of the board could leave an ugly mark.

4 Mark the dimensions of the window in pencil. If you are going to cut the bevel with a trimming-knife, a type with snap-off blades is best. Be careful, once you have cut the board, the edges can be extremely sharp.

5 The tip of the blade should be placed just to the outside edge of the pencil line so you can see as you cut. Cut against the beveled side of the steel rule, holding the knife at what you judge to be an angle of 60°. The pencil line should be visible on the edge of the cut out window – the center part.

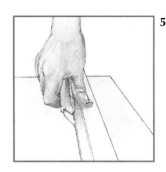

6 Push the tip of the blade into the full depth of the board, starting at the top of the line you are cutting, and then, with a tense arm, pull the blade down the length of the line toward your body. Remove the knife cleanly from the board.

7 Turn the board 90° and repeat the procedure for the next cut. You should finish the cut slightly beyond the point where the lines cross each other.

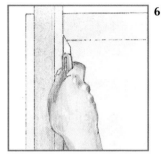

8 When you have made all four cuts, the center should drop out cleanly. It may not always do this immediately, so you may need to re-insert the blade, or use an artist's scalpel to nick each corner to release the center. Eventually, you will be able to judge when and where to stop each cut for the center to come away cleanly.

Cutting oval or round bevelled matts is a little harder, although if you have a bevel matt-cutter it will be somewhat easier. Professionals use a special piece of equipment.

You could however, use a dish, platter, or similar household item as a guide. Use it to make a template and then use this to cut around. You will need to practice to achieve a smooth curve.

You can buy ready-cut oval and circular matts as well as prepared matts for framing a number of pictures together – for example, sets of postcards or family photographs.

NEXT PAGE: An attractive selection of completed decorative matts and frames.

MOUNTING PICTURES

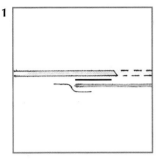

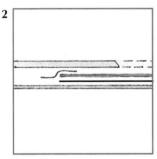

If you want to avoid your pictures wrinkling inside the frame, you will need to secure them to a light cardboard in some way. Here are just a few variations.

Method One

Dry-mounting uses a special adhesive sheet, sandwiched between the artwork and the matt cardboard – usually white $1/32$in cardboard. Specially-treated release paper is used with each sheet to protect the face of the picture from the heat.

Always ensure the picture is completely clean and free from dust and grease, or bubbles and tiny dents can appear.

Bonding takes place when the press reaches the correct temperature, sealing the artwork and the cardboard together.

Run strips of acid-free tape around the perimeter of the picture attached to the matt for long term strength.

1 Most professionals choose to "dry-mount" pictures which are not originals to the back of the matt – using a special dry-mount press.

2 Alternatively "dry-mount" pictures to a separate backing cardboard, then position the matt over the picture.

Method Two

You can utilize the adhesive sheets without a dry-mount press using a warm iron.

3 Cut the adhesive sheet to the same size as the picture, place it on the back of the picture and, lifting the picture away for a moment, touch the adhesive sheet in the center with a warm iron so it attaches to the back of the picture.

4 Place this – with the picture face up in position on the backing-cardboard – and again lightly touch the adhesive sheet with a warm iron to attach it to the cardboard.

Just attach it at one point only as more may cause bubbling.

5 Then place the protective sheet over the picture and iron gently from the center. Keep the iron very cool to start with, working up to the correct temperature to bond the picture in position.

Dry-mount presses vary in size. If you use a small 13in x 16in area press, it will be necessary to reposition the picture within the press several times to cover the total area.

Method Three

You may also make a hinged matt, using a piece of cardboard the same size as the already-cut matt.

6 Trim a piece of cardboard the same size as the cut matt, lay the two together on a flat surface, and run a strip of masking tape across the join so that the matt hinges open.

7 Place the picture between the hinged, already-cut matt and backing-cardboard. Position the picture accurately within the matt window.

8 Ideally, use two small pieces of gummed, acid-free tape which will not mark the original artwork, and stick them to the back of the artwork so they extend slightly. Then secure these crosswise to the backing cardboard with either masking or gummed tape .

Another alternative, although not recommended, is to glue the picture to the backing cardboard. However, beware using anything too wet (such as wallpaper paste) which can soak into the picture and cause it to bubble or damage it more severely. Cans of "spray-mount" are more suitable.

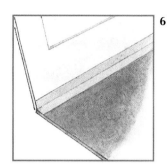

6

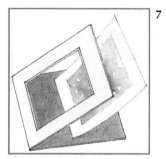

7

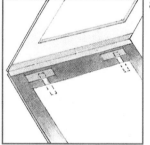

8

BUYING AND CUTTING GLASS

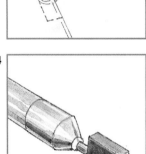

1

4

Glass is usually sold in sheets which can be rather awkward to handle and store but most suppliers will sell cut sheets and will deliver them to you for a charge.

You may prefer to have glass cut to size by a local glass-supplier. If you do, measure the area of the frame into which the picture will fit exactly and the glass cutter will make the correct allowance for a comfortable fit, or ideally take the frame, matt, and picture with you.

There are several types of glass available, the most widely used being $1/16$in paper float. You may occasionally find a use for non-reflective glass which is more expensive than paper float and has the unfortunate effect of dulling the picture slightly. Its main advantage is that it enables you to look at the picture instead of yourself if the picture is hung in a brightly-lit room.

1 Trying to fit a piece of glass into a frame which is slightly too small can lead to a nasty accident later when the glass cracks from too much pressure. It is also an awfully tricky job trimming a slim strip of glass from an already cut piece, although it can be done by nibbling it away with special glass (grozling) pliers.

It is quite easy to cut your own glass once you have the knack although even the experts have their disasters!

2 Ensure you have a flat surface wide enough to take the full size of the sheet of glass – none should extend over the edge or you will be unable to cut correctly.

3 You can only cut glass in straight complete lines; it is not possible to turn corners in one single cut.

4 You will need a glass-cutter, either with a tungsten wheel containing lubricating oil in the handle helping it run more smoothly, or a cutter which has to be lubricated by dipping it regularly into a sponge pad containing cutting-oil or white spirit. The latter will not last quite so long and does not have such a good cutting edge.

5 Make sure you have a completely clean surface to work on, perhaps with some cushioning of newspaper or felt under a heavy cardboard working surface, and mark the size needed on the glass with a fine felt-tip pen or colored chinagraph (wax) pencil. It is a good idea to practice the technique first on small pieces of glass rather than waste larger pieces.

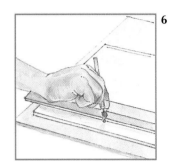

6 Use a long steel ruler to cut against and ensure the cutter is exactly on the line you have drawn. You will not be cutting right through the glass, simply scoring it.

Let the wheel of the cutter run, keeping your fingers straight, pressing firmly and continuously, starting at the top of the line and drawing it down toward you. The pressure should come from your shoulder, not your wrist.

You will be able to hear it scoring the surface and the noise should sound fluid rather than crunchy; the latter indicates you are using too much pressure and crushing the glass.

7 The technique now is to break the glass cleanly along the line. Pull the glass over the edge of the table enough to get a grip with your thumbs, one each side of the cut line.

The thumbs should almost touch each other and your fingers should be underneath the glass. Lift the glass up slightly – half an inch or so – and at the same time, twist your hands away from each other, pushing up with the two fingers under the glass. Watch the glass split – hopefully – down the line.

CUTTING THE BACKBOARD

Probably the easiest task is cutting the hardboard backing. You should use ¹/₁₆in hardboard for the backboard, ideally a new type called SBS (smooth both sides) which is half the thickness of ordinary hardboard. Although not generally available, it can be bought from framing suppliers. It can be cut with a trimming-knife or a miter-saw if you find it easier.

Do not try to cut right through with a knife – just score it, then snap it, using a fine rasp to tidy up the edges.

If you cut the hardboard with a saw, smooth the edges down with some sandpaper, or again use a fine rasp.

The hardboard backing should fit snugly into the back of the frame and be pinned in as part of the sandwich at the very end of the process. Before doing this the fittings for the backing should be attached (see page 35).

On some occasions, particularly if the rabbet of the frame is shallow, it may be necessary to chamfer the edges and drive the pins or staples into the frame at an angle (see page 32).

You now have the four lengths of mitered molding, the beveled matt, the glass, the back-board, and the mounted picture.

The next step is to make up the frame. Double-check that everything is going to fit within the frame first by making it up as a "dummy" run.

BELOW: Bring all the elements together for final assembly.

MAKING UP THE FRAME

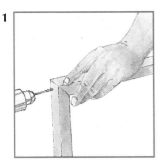

Professional framers use an expensive piece of equipment called an underpinner. It employs air pressure to shoot pins into the frame from the back to reinforce the corners. However, the home-framer will use panel pins which are hammered into the sides of the frame.

Do not put the pins in from the top or bottom of the frame as the weight of the glass, matt, and backing may be too great, and may force the frame apart.

You will need two pins at each corner (unless the frame is too narrow and there is only room for one) so it is recommended that you drill the holes for the pins first, using a narrow bit in a hand-drill so that the pin is a tight fit. Only drill the upright leg, not the leg the pin is being driven into.

It is advisable to glue and pin the corners as you go.

1 Take length 1 (long) and length 3 (short) and check that the mitered corners fit neatly together. Pre-drill the holes for the pins in the upright leg and knock the pins in halfway.

2 Smear a touch of wood-glue on the two mitered faces. Clamp the first leg in position. Then, putting the two faces together and ensuring the joint is good, clamp the second leg in place. Wipe off any excess glue that squeezes out.

3 Hit the pins home using a small hammer and, using a nail-set, punch them so they disappear just below the surface of the wood. Later, you can fill the dent with wood-filler or wax which can be retouched with matching paint on a very thin brush, or even a water-based, colored pencil. Leave to set.

4 Do the same with lengths 2 and 4. Then repeat the process with 1 and 4, and 2 and 3.

5 You will need four corner-clamps to hold the corners in the correct position. If you only have one or two clamps, you can do it in stages.

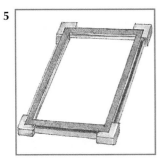

To hold the complete frame firmly, use a tape clamp. Ensure this fits straight and holds the frame without twisting. Use the winder which is incorporated in one of the corners to wind the tape so that it holds the corners firmly.

FINAL ASSEMBLY

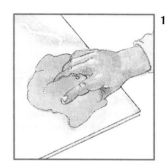

Having given the frame plenty of time for the glue to set, make sure your working area is clean. The first task is to carefully clean the glass. There is nothing more infuriating than putting together a picture which you then find has a large speck of dust just behind the glass!

1 Rest the glass on a piece of felt or similar smooth cloth, use a glass-cleaning spray to clean both sides carefully with a soft lint-free cloth or paper towel (it is dust-free, disposable, and inexpensive), ensuring there are no smears.

2 Brush any loose chippings or sawdust out of the rabbet of the frame and any specks of dust you can see on the matt or picture itself.

3 Find a shallow box, smaller than the overall picture. Place the picture with the attached matt, then the glass (taking care to place the glass on the picture directly rather than pushing it across) then the frame on top, gently adjusting it all into the correct position. Turn the thing over and place the hardboard backing into the recess.

Use either of the following methods to attach the hardboard backing to the frame.

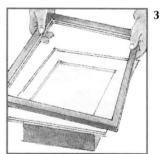

4 Professional framers use a staple-gun which shoots flat, metal, diamond- or arrow-shaped pins into the inside edge of the frame, pressing the hardboard to the rest of the picture sandwich and holding it all in place.

5 Alternatively, you can hammer in fine panel-pins. They need to be driven into the inside edge of the frame with a hammer, so that the length of the pin slides across the backing board, sandwiching it tightly.

Whichever method you use, do not scrimp on pins; use several along each length at regular intervals.

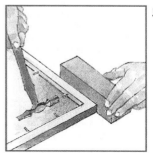

As they are inserted, hold a heavy weight (a padded wooden block or lead weight) against the outside edge of the frame to absorb the shock waves.

If it is not possible for the back-board to fit flush into the frame, chamfer the edges of the board so that you can drive the pins into the frame at an angle.

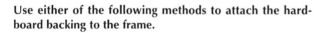

THE FINISHING TOUCH

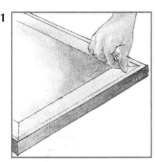

Once you have pinned the frame together, there is some tidying up to do.

1 Cover the pins holding the back of the frame with strips of either self-adhesive brown paper tape or masking tape, mitering the corners for neatness.

A craft-knife is the best way of cutting the tape – just a nick to the corner gives you a nice neat edge. The tape will also help to keep out dust and insects.

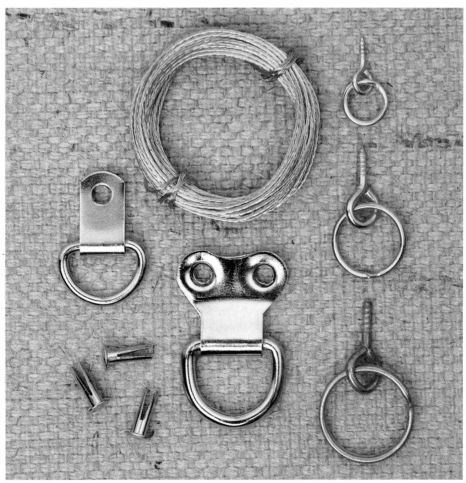

HANGING METHODS

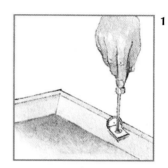

Which fastenings you use to hang your picture depends on its size. Two screw-eyes and a length of nylon cord will not be adequate to support a large poster but perfectly suitable for a small (10in x 8in) watercolor.

The best type of fittings are D-rings which are riveted to the backboard about a fifth of the way in from the side of the frame. Alternatively, screw-eyes with a ring for the cord or wire are screwed to the frame but may not be suitable for very narrow frames.

1 Position the fittings about a third of the way down from the top of the picture (D-rings should be fitted to the backboard before your final assembly of the picture) but can also be riveted to the frame.

2 Take a length of picture-hanging wire or nylon cord and run it between the D-rings or screw-eyes, allowing a little take-up (not too much) by pushing the wire upward with your finger at the center point to approximately two inches from the top of the picture.

3 Tie a double knot through one D-ring and run the wire across to the other D-ring.

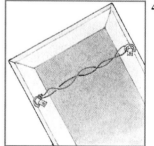

4 Return the wire across, twisting the two lengths together to strengthen the cord. Secure the twisted wire through the D-ring at the other end.

The wall fixing could be as simple as a picture hook or nail, although once again it depends on the size of the picture and to some extent the type of wall. For larger pictures, it is safer to use an anchor and screw or masonry nail if you are attaching a hook to an outside brick or an internal load-bearing wall.

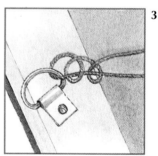

OPPOSITE: A selection of fastenings for hanging.

HANGING PICTURES CREATIVELY

Give some careful thought to your picture display. A small picture hung in the center of a large wall will look totally lost.

You may feel that the pictures you hang are likely to stay in one place for some time or at least until the room is redecorated, but it is worth considering having the flexibility to change them around or replace them with new ones. Grouping pictures together allows you to do this.

Do not dismiss the more unusual rooms of the house. The bathroom, the kitchen, and the cloakroom all deserve enlivening and often have unusually-shaped areas where a picture will fit neatly.

However, beware of hanging delicate watercolors or oils in steamy places, such as near the bathtub or shower, or in the kitchen. They could be damaged by the humidity.

Other unusual places include over doorways, on the backs of doors, under sloping roofs (as long as it is bright enough) and in recesses alongside chimney breasts.

You can hang a picture alone (if it is striking enough) complemented by the furniture around it – why not place it on an easel, on a mantelpiece, or in a recess?

There is no need for a pair of pictures to be on the same theme although this can work. If you treat them similarly, with the same frame and matt, they can hang together very well.

No need for them to be hung exactly side by side, either. One a third higher than the other, with about a third of the width between them, will balance nicely. A table positioned centrally beneath gives more symmetry.

Nor is there any reason why pictures of different shapes, even ovals, cannot be hung together in a group.

If you take a line as eye-level, try and arrange the pictures centered along this line or above and below it. Alternatively, you can take an imaginary square, cross, or rectangle and build the pictures within this.

Ideally, keep larger pictures at the top of the arrangement and smaller pictures below where they can be seen more easily.

OPPOSITE ABOVE: A wall covered with pictures can look stunning.

OPPOSITE BELOW: Creative picture-hanging on a sloped wall adds interest to a room.

Elizabeth Whiting Associates

Elizabeth Whiting Associates

CREATIVE FRAMING

A few simple but effective framing variations.

DECORATIVE MATTS

There are many ways to decorate a basic matt but you can also add a complementary touch by picking out a color from your picture in a second matt which slips beneath the main matt to make a slim, colored border.

CUTTING A DOUBLE MATT

1 Cut the window to fit the picture in the first matt using colored cardboard.

2 Select a second piece of cardboard in a complimentary color to the first and trim the outside measurements to exactly the same as the first.

3 Cut out the second matt's window around a 1/4in larger than for the first matt. This measurement can vary, either smaller or larger, depending on your taste.

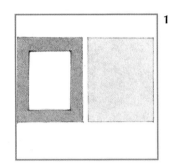

The middle section of the first matt can be dropped onto the marked-out second matt to check that both are square and that the width is equal all the way around.

4 Cut out the window of the second matt and place the frame on top of the first matt.

5 Using double-sided tape, carefully stick the two matts together to finish the completed double matt.

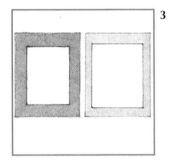

You can use the same procedure for making a triple matt – perhaps varying the width of the third matt – but check that the depth of the rabbet on the frame is deep enough to accommodate them all!

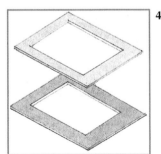

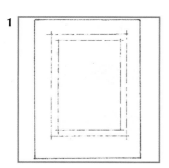

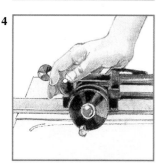

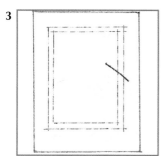

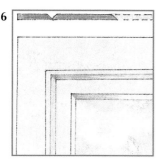

CUTTING A V-GROOVE BORDER

One popular way to decorate a matt is to cut a V-groove. Cut the overall size of the matt cardboard as you would for a single matt.

1 Draw on the back the size you need for the final window – say 2in at the top and sides but 3in at the bottom.

2 Then draw another rectangle around that, half an inch (or whatever you decide) closer to the outside edge – 1½in at the top and sides and 2½in at the bottom.

3 Draw a pencil line on the back from the edge to near the center so you can replace the cut-out piece the same way up, using the pencil line as a guide for re-positioning.

4 Cut the outside window first, which forms the cut for the V-groove. Drop the window out, turn it over, face up, and cut the bevel at the same angle as you did from the back. Be careful not to cut too much off.

V-grooves are better cut with the proper hand tools.

5 Replace the center piece inside the matt, face down, ensure the pencil line you drew aligns on both pieces, and tape the two together at the back, using masking tape.

6 Cut the final window which will frame your picture. The result will be the nice effect of a V-groove half an inch away from the picture.

DECORATIVE RULES AND BORDERS

Another way of adding a border is to use a ruling-pen, filled with gold-colored or other colored paint.

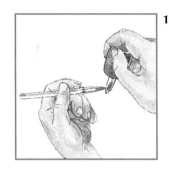

1 Use a pen which allows you to adjust the thickness of the rule and which has a wide nib so you can hold enough ink. Draw your border lightly in pencil before attempting the real thing.

2 You can then fill the borders, using watercolor wash, applied with a sable brush.

If you want to experiment with this technique there is a kit available which uses powder rather than paint and has all you need to add wash-line decoration to your matts.

The kit includes a corner-gauge which enables you to decide where the rules will fall and accurately mark them out (see figure 1, page 42).

BELOW: A sample of matts with an effective use of rules and borders.

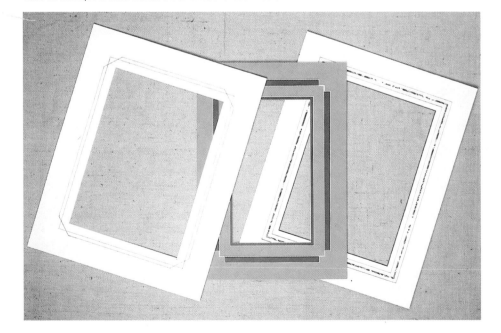

A WASHED LINE MATT

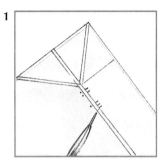

1 Mark an inside and outside ink border, of one or several lines, using a ruling pen and creating a central area which will be filled with color.

2 Using a straight edge (ruler) draw up the straight lines to link the marked out points.

3 Using an artist's sable brush, load the brush with color and lightly guide a wet line wash evenly between the marked-up lines.

If you are not sure about your drawing talent, there are plenty of other methods of decorating matts including matt-decoration papers.

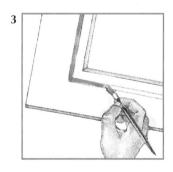

MATT-DECORATION PAPERS – are thin paper veneers which can be cut from sheets and stuck on with double-sided tape, or supplied with a self-adhesive backing in continuous rolls in a range of designs including marbled, wash and line, antique gold and silver, or plain pastels. Corner designs like stencils are also available in this self-adhesive format – or you could use a stencil kit and choose your own colors.

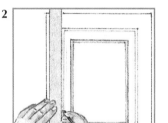

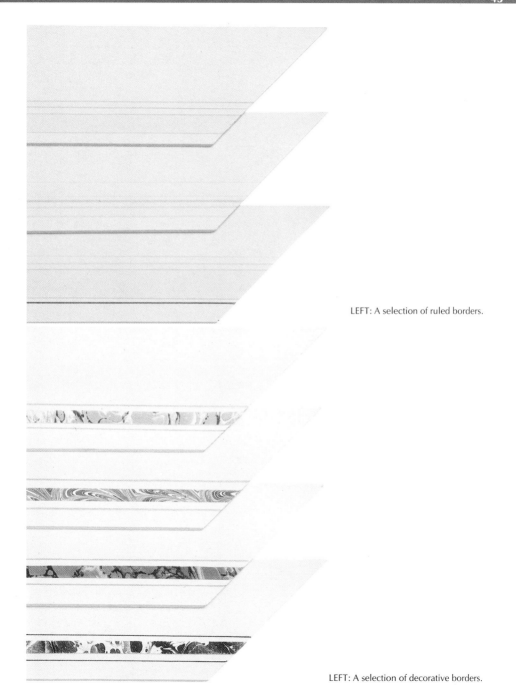

LEFT: A selection of ruled borders.

LEFT: A selection of decorative borders.

DECORATIVE FRAMES

The introduction of plain wood frames has opened up all kinds of possibilities for decorative finishes.

You may wish to show the wood-grain off to its full advantage, either staining it with one of the wide range of water – or spirit-based – wood-stain colors that are now available, varnishing it, then brushing on a clear shellac to seal it and give a sheen or gloss finish depending on how many coats you apply.

Alternatively you can use paint to create some stippled or ragged effects using the same techniques as you would on walls or furniture.

For the more adventurous, it is not so difficult to re-create the effects of marble and tortoise shell which can look particularly stunning when used to frame mirrors and oil-paintings.

It is always helpful to have a sample of the marble or tortoise shell on hand (or a picture if the real thing is not available).

You will need:
PLAIN WOOD MOLDING – preferably not too grained or knotty.
UNIVERSAL PRIMER – or sanding sealer.
EGGSHELL PAINT.
WET-AND-DRY SANDPAPER.
ARTIST'S PAINTS.
CAN OF TRANSPARENT GLAZE.
BRUSHES – a selection including fitches, a hogshair softening brush, a Japanese Hakka and a small domed-sash or similar brush for tapping on paint.
MASKING TAPE.
ARTIST'S PALETTE – make your own with a piece of hardboard covered in parchment paper.

First prepare the frame with the universal primer (or sanding sealer). Build up several layers of eggshell paint (six should do it) and sand it down to a very smooth finish with wet-and-dry sandpaper.

Work on one leg of the frame at a time, covering the mitered corner with masking tape to ensure a clean line.

MARBLING

The two artist's colors we suggest you start with are Payne's gray and raw umber, but you can vary these and add extra colors once you have perfected the technique.

1 Apply a very thin coat of transparent glaze to the first leg of the frame. Then "tap" on the gray using the domed-sash or other small brush evenly over the entire surface. Do not make it too dark.

2 Use the hogshair softening brush to soften the surface color – you will be surprised at how marble-like the effect is already.

3 If you do not like the effect in any particular area, dab it with a rag and soften again with the hogshair brush. Then "tap" the raw umber along the edges of the gray paint, picking out the shapes that suggest themselves. Skim gently over this with the hogshair brush and blend the two colors gently with a fitch brush.

4 To add the veins, use a fine pointed brush and trickle in the brown (raw umber) paint along routes which suggest themselves, such as the edges of the raw umber. Do not overdo it, but link the veins as you go along.

5 Splatter some white spirit onto the paint with a fitch to create some interesting teardrop effects and colorings.

BELOW: A selection of decorative frames including marbled and limed frames.

TORTOISE SHELLING

You can imitate the shell of a turtle (called tortoise shell) using a similar techniques.

1 Apply a thin coat of transparent glaze to the prepared frame.

2 Mix equal parts of raw sienna and yellow ocher with a touch of glaze.

3 Tap the color evenly onto the prepared frame with a stippling action. Do not make it too thick or the paint will streak when you soften it.

4 Mix some burnt umber with a touch of glaze. Add little dabs to the stippled base with a fitch brush. Imagine that you are painting little groups of grains – not quite touching each other.

5 A pattern begins to emerge – watch out for edges and open spaces.

6 Soften the edges with a hogshair softening brush, closing up the shapes where they appear.

7 Using the darker raw umber and with a second fitch brush, add highlights where they suggest themselves.

8 Soften the whole with a Hakka, which gives a smoother effect than that of the hogshair softening brush.

A wide range of other effects can be achieved and you can take classes in these techniques if this sort of decoration appeals to you. You can re-create malachite, lapis lazuli, birds-eye maple, and red leather to name but a few.

MARBLING

The two artist's colors we suggest you start with are Payne's gray and raw umber, but you can vary these and add extra colors once you have perfected the technique.

1 Apply a very thin coat of transparent glaze to the first leg of the frame. Then "tap" on the gray using the domed-sash or other small brush evenly over the entire surface. Do not make it too dark.

2 Use the hogshair softening brush to soften the surface color – you will be surprised at how marble-like the effect is already.

3 If you do not like the effect in any particular area, dab it with a rag and soften again with the hogshair brush. Then "tap" the raw umber along the edges of the gray paint, picking out the shapes that suggest themselves. Skim gently over this with the hogshair brush and blend the two colors gently with a fitch brush.

4 To add the veins, use a fine pointed brush and trickle in the brown (raw umber) paint along routes which suggest themselves, such as the edges of the raw umber. Do not overdo it, but link the veins as you go along.

5 Splatter some white spirit onto the paint with a fitch to create some interesting teardrop effects and colorings.

BELOW: A selection of decorative frames including marbled and limed frames.

TORTOISE SHELLING

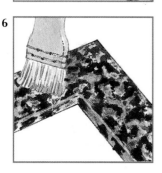

1

You can imitate the shell of a turtle (called tortoise shell) using a similar techniques.

1 Apply a thin coat of transparent glaze to the prepared frame.

2 Mix equal parts of raw sienna and yellow ocher with a touch of glaze.

3 Tap the color evenly onto the prepared frame with a stippling action. Do not make it too thick or the paint will streak when you soften it.

4 Mix some burnt umber with a touch of glaze. Add little dabs to the stippled base with a fitch brush. Imagine that you are painting little groups of grains – not quite touching each other.

5 A pattern begins to emerge – watch out for edges and open spaces.

6 Soften the edges with a hogshair softening brush, closing up the shapes where they appear.

7 Using the darker raw umber and with a second fitch brush, add highlights where they suggest themselves.

8 Soften the whole with a Hakka, which gives a smoother effect than that of the hogshair softening brush.

A wide range of other effects can be achieved and you can take classes in these techniques if this sort of decoration appeals to you. You can re-create malachite, lapis lazuli, birds-eye maple, and red leather to name but a few.

Photographic props supplied by:

Nina Barough Styling

As credited, photographic material reproduced by kind permission of:

Elizabeth Whiting Associates